Stories That Matter

The Everyday Stories of Extraordinary Business Owners

Mike Garner

Stories That Matter Publishing

For Jan (she knows)

For Jo Howarth, who cleared my mind, for Margo Aaron, who set me on the path and for Vicky Quinn Fraser, who held my feet to the fire.

Contents

This book is for you ...

If you think you have nothing to say. If you think no one will be interested in you. If you want to say something meaningful but don't know where to start. If you think your story isn't all that relevant anyway, you just want to get on with marketing your business. If you've ever watched other business owners forge ahead of you full of confidence, even though you know your offer and expertise are better than theirs.

I was like you once. I hesitated to say what I thought. It's time for you and me to have a voice. It's time for us to tell our everyday stories because they are the stories of our lives.

This book has had so many false starts I've lost count. I've sat down at a desk and not gotten past the first page, the first few lines. I abandoned projects as soon as they got a little tricky, and the self-doubt set in.

Who the hell am I to be writing a book, anyway? I have nothing to say. Apart from upping sticks and living in a foreign country for half my life and going native, surviving 25 years of self-employment in two countries, and having one of the most romantic hookups you could ever imagine in my forties, that is. No, apart from that, nothing.

I never gave up the idea of telling my story—and neither should you. This book tells the stories of people, for the most part, you've never heard of. But they are just like you. They run businesses; they have lives, struggles, and victories. They put themselves out there; they're sometimes brave and sometimes not, but they all show up.

I make no apologies about it being a collection of stories, the testimonies and experiences of the people I like. If you're inspired to think about doing more to tell yours, I'll take it as a victory.

Who the hell am I to write a book?

In January 2020, my brother, my wife and I decided that my mother could no longer cope at home alone. Her advancing Alzheimer's disease had made her a danger to herself. She needed help.

She'd lost most of her mobility and speech, but I think she still had most of her mind. She'd have conversations with us, happy in her little world and convinced we could understand her. But we could hardly understand a word she said.

A week later, when I was visiting my mother in the home in London, my wife Jan had a letter from doctors inviting her back for a second mammogram because they'd found something suspicious in the first one. She should expect it to be cancer. It was.

The year started with a bang. We'd already spent Christmas and the New Year with coughs and fevers, the significance of which we didn't realise till later in the year. She had the operation and is fine now, but it was a bumpy ride at the time.

I went to see my mother at the end of February and I think

she was happy. Never one to be physically demonstrative, she touched me a lot, smiled all the time and told anyone who'd listen that I was her boy. Sixty-one years old, but I was still her boy. That was the last time I saw her.

Falls had landed her in hospital several times over the previous eighteen months, but she had a bad one in May. She broke ribs on both sides, cracked her cheekbone and hit her head sufficiently hard to get a bleed on the brain. She must have gone down like a sack of spuds.

A bleed on the brain is never a good thing for otherwise healthy people, but at the age of 87, she would not have survived the operation. I had to tell the doctor to release her from hospital for palliative care as she was drifting in and out of consciousness and wasn't going to improve. She died on the morning of 21st June, the day after Jan's 60th birthday.

Jan also had (planned) heart surgery and a couple of blackouts that got her driving licence suspended for a year. I don't want this to descend into self-pity because it's not that kind of story, but we packed a lot into the first half of 2020.

When you're in the middle of a sequence of events like that, you just ride with the punches. You wonder what will happen next, but you keep going. It's only afterwards you think, "what the hell was that?" and "what do I do now?"

When it was all over, I thought about who I was and where I was going. Sorting out the probate was the final curtain on my previous life and I was now at the top of the genealogical pile. My brother and I and our two grown-up children were the only ones left. I have two older cousins in the US and three step-children, but that was all that remained of my direct family line. I no longer had parents to refer to. I was on my own. That felt strangely liberating and scary.

It was time to work out what I wanted to do when I grew

up. I was no longer playing. My mother was 26 when I was born, I had to decide what to do with the years left to me.

Losing two close family members—my uncle died in November 2019—and seeing your wife and teenage sweetheart (more on that later) having to face up to her mortality makes you think. Maybe all those things I might have feared in the past weren't worth the bother?

I've spent a lifetime plagued with a lack of self-belief and self-esteem, along with imagined guilt and shame. Brené Brown says that guilt is saying "I did that", and shame is saying "I am that." I was that failure. My flagging self-belief stopped me from doing many things I'd love to have done, like becoming an architect or a history professor. It almost stopped me from writing this book. But you're reading it now, proof that I beat the little sod. I've spent a lifetime getting ready to be successful. "I just need to do this thing, and I'll be successful", "I just need to get this qualification and...", "I just have to do...", you get the picture.

I've wanted to write a book for as long as I can remember. I produced a couple of short stories in my twenties and tried several times in the subsequent years, but never got past the first paragraph.

More recently, I made several more serious attempts and wrote a few thousand words. But imposter syndrome and a lack of good ideas always got in the way. The world doesn't need another book about copywriting, especially from me. And I didn't want to write it, anyway.

I thought I'd drifted through life with nothing extraordinary to show for it. I dreamed of playing football for England as a kid. That wasn't happening, even in my remotest of fantasies. I haven't found a cure for cancer and haven't had the star corporate career I watched so many of my peers achieve over the years. I also missed several of my ambitions. I wanted to be an architect, a history professor and (briefly) an interior designer. All consigned to the graveyard of my life goals.

I had plenty of layers of shame to pull back. It's a pernicious little bastard that gets you when you are mostly unaware, creeping up on you, then crushing you without you realising what it's doing.

I consider myself one of the lucky ones because I realised it before it was too late. I niggled away at those "you'll never make it" moments, and those "is that all you've done with your life despite all the potential you had?" moments or those "you're not good enough to mix with these people" moments.

I did some work with my friend Margo Aaron at the end of 2020. She got me writing properly and without a filter. It's as though she opened up the floodgates and the words just came thundering through.

So I wrote, but not with fear as I'd tried in the past. I wrote with total honesty. I had conversations with myself like I'd never had before. I wrote down memories, feelings and regrets some of which will never see the light of day. They'd been rattling around in my head for decades, but just writing them down—sometimes quite literally by hand—was an effective way of putting them to rest.

The effect was to tell me I had a story to tell. I had value and experience people wanted to hear. That was the lightbulb moment that started everything.

Margo also encouraged me to do Seth Godin's altMBA. I'd seen the website and the videos of the people saying how it had transformed them and thought, "that's way above my pay grade", but there I was, applying and getting in; I'm not sure I recognised myself.

And, of course, it transformed me. I met tremendous people

I would never have met otherwise, resulting in a complete system upgrade. I told people from across the world I was going to write a book and they told me they wanted to read it. I interviewed some of them for it and they all said they were honoured to talk to me. A couple even confessed to imposter syndrome while talking to me.

You what? Have I landed on another planet? I'm the one who's supposed to have imposter syndrome, not you. Well, I guess I'm better at this stuff than I thought.

So, that is the backstory behind this book. I've talked to business owners and others, not at all like me. Their stories are sometimes dramatic, sometimes quite mundane. Some were determined to run their business from day one; others drifted into it almost accidentally. Many, like me, have experienced doubt while others don't know what that word means (lucky sods).

We are blessed by not having to do the nine-to-five. We are outliers; we are taking a stand. Even in the most challenging moments, when things are going as badly as they could when we think we might want to jack it in and go and stack shelves in a supermarket. Even in those moments, we realise we can take a Thursday afternoon off, and no boss can do anything about it. That is priceless because it means we are in control.

Ash Ambirge lost three parents—her two birth parents and her stepfather by the time she was legally entitled to vote. She fended off the lecherous attentions of potential clients, an uncaring administration and domestic abuse to become an insanely successful copywriter.

Jo Howarth's parents divorced when she was in primary school. She grew up feeling it was her fault and fearing an often violent and serially unfaithful stepfather. In early adulthood, she repeated the patterns of bad relationships and abuse until she found the therapy and loving family that helped her build a business in mental health that is helping hundreds of others.

One of the first things Kira Hug told me was that she has suffered no real drama in her life. But she always knew she'd be a business owner one day—she didn't know how she was going to do it. There's a direct line between her being president of her sorority at Virginia Tech and running with a business partner on one of the world's biggest podcasts and communities of copywriters.

Margo Aaron always felt she was a square peg in a round hole in her corporate life. She'd been brought up to think independently and couldn't reconcile the need to be creative and tow the company line simultaneously. Since she's been a freelancer, she's built a business that has put her into the worlds of some of the greatest marketers alive, and she works very much on her terms.

Unlike me, self-doubt has never been an issue for Michelle Dalley. She left school at 16 because she wanted to work and has been doing that ever since. Not at all a square peg in a round hole, she loved the corporate life. She only left when she decided she didn't want to miss any milestones in her new son's life. She grew a business in food marketing with her husband, using the skills she built in her corporate life. I've never seen her without a smile on her face.

We get into business for all kinds of reasons. No two stories of the people in this book are the same. There is joy; there is despair. It is impossible to explain why we do it to someone who isn't in the arena with us.

So, these are our stories. We remain in control. Whatever our journey, one thing unites us; we're just trying to do our bit to make the world a better place.

Chapter 1

Why Thinking You Have Nothing To Say Is Just Plain Wrong

"I don't know how interesting my story is"

That's what James Hutchinson said to me when I asked him if I could interview him for this book. He had no idea why I'd want to talk to him. Nothing to say? Are you kidding? He'd had an epiphany. Wait until you hear the details.

James is in his mid-forties and starting his third business as a direct result of the events of the last couple of years. He sold the first one and left the second to whither on the vine of the pandemic. It could have sustained him for many years, but his heart wasn't in it anymore.

People think their stories are nothing extraordinary because they're right in the middle of them. They live their lives from the inside; they live what they perceive to be "normal."

We deal poorly with ostentation. The British are perhaps world champions at trying to knock people down once they've become successful. Our parents and teachers told us when we were younger not to draw attention to ourselves because "nobody likes a show-off."A classic, almost uniquely British putdown is that "he's a bit full of himself." So maybe it's natural that James should say he's not extraordinary.

The new business started with a moment of panic one day because he couldn't find a suit for a funeral he was attending. He spent an entire day looking around Glasgow's shops and could not find anything that his 54 or 56-inch chest—he's not sure how big he was—would fit. He only found three in the world's largest menswear store with 200,000 suits over 5,000 square feet. The situation was untenable; he had to do something.

So, he embarked on an intensive weight loss programme and went from 24 stone or somewhere north of 330 pounds to

16 stone or 220 pounds, transforming his life. Not just in terms of his physical health but also from a mental and mindset perspective.

He started taking pride in the way he dressed and gained some self-respect. "I am never going to be Orlando Bloom", he says. And neither does he want to be. "But I can be the best version of me"

Later, he was at a conference where people kept telling him how well he'd done. James is not a man to accept praise easily; it makes him quite uncomfortable. But the sheer weight of numbers made him think there must be something in it. He had achieved something great, and perhaps he could pass on what he had learned to others. His wife Carla, never one to mince her words with him, told him just to say "thank you" and move on.

The pandemic allowed him to start afresh. He trained as a stylist and set up a clothing and accessories business for middle-aged men who want to look and feel better. "I like to look dapper", he says.

He's setting up physical stores in Carlisle where he lives and Glasgow where he was born. He's planning a network of them across the world.

James has found his purpose and is dreaming big. He wants a brand to rival the big boys. His sense of purpose is such that I find it difficult to argue with him.

He's a little less convinced he has nothing interesting to say now. He realises his work is meaningful. James is like many business owners I've met over the years. They're conditioned not to blow their own trumpet by their "I know my place" working-class roots and to get on with life. They go to work, come home to play and relax, and don't fuss. They spend their lives failing to realise how extraordinary they are. Let's tell some of their stories.

Your life is boring, and it's just as well

Imagine what it would be like if we all lived like Jack Bauer in 24? Or *Buffy the Vampire Slayer*? Or Sandra Bullock and Keanu Reeves in *Speed*? Our lives would be white-knuckle rides of fun and probably quite unbearable.

Here's a scoop; those stories are not real. They're full of actors pretending. Do you seriously believe that old Jack goes through all that tension without needing the toilet just once? Or didn't anyone notice the extraordinarily high death rate among teens in Sunnydale, CA and the school collapsing not once but twice? Real life isn't like that. Even those of us who have the most "fun" have lives of contrast. We live in a binary world where being happy only exists in relation to being sad, good exists in relation to bad, and fun only exists in relation to boredom.

Most people's lives are mundane. I don't think many of us would survive the emotional upset of the lives of most of our fictional characters.

Despite what Instagram or TikTok might tell you, we spend our time getting up, going to work on a train, a bus, or a car and coming home again the same way. Outside of work, we can spend our time on our own or with friends. We muddle through as we can with our day-to-day concerns. We watch TV, clean the house, eat everyday things, and go out occasionally.

We ask questions such as, "Where's the money gone this month?", "What's for tea?" or "What are we doing at the weekend?" That's how most of our lives go.

But these things are what make up the stories and

narratives we tell ourselves all the time. They are important because they are what bring us together as human beings. Everyone experiences them, making them mundane but intensely human at the same time.

After early protohumans developed speech and groupings grew beyond the domination of the local alpha male into societies, they needed to find a way to bind themselves together and avoid descending into anarchy.

That tool was initially gossip—individuals talking behind the backs of others about others—which soon developed into stories. That's where the great myths and great religions come from, but it's also where the bland comes from; smaller, more mundane stories we tell each other every day are born. Those stories have continued to drive the human experience and make us relatable. Someone will be interested in what you have to say. They are what make us attractive to others. Your tribe is there.

Meaning, purpose and why are we here?

The need to know where we come from, who we are and where we're going goes back to before the hunter-gatherers and to the earliest Homo Sapiens. They lived in the moment without memory. If one of them got trapped by the jaws of the sabre-tooth tiger, it would cause much consternation. As soon as the event was over, they'd forget.

As their brains evolved, they realised that if others died, it stood to reason that one day, they would too. Which begged the question, "what's the point in going out to get food every day if we're going to die, anyway?" That was the first philosophical question ever asked, "what is the point of all this?" The answer was that they weren't just hunting for themselves. They were hunting for the community as a whole and the greater good. As well as solving the question of the meaning of life, they'd found a sense of purpose.

Your story and purpose go together. The more you remember and reflect, the more meaning and challenges will become apparent. "Meaningful" work isn't about one job being worth more than another; it's not a competition. You don't want teachers competing with doctors and nurses for public sympathy, especially in a post-pandemic world. No one will argue caregivers or teachers don't do worthwhile work. The issue is the meaning that you find in your work.

Most of us crave meaningful work. Especially if we run a business, we want to know that we make an impact on our customers and the wider community. Purpose and meaning are the centres of authentic communication that resonates with a target audience.

In *The Psychology of Working*, David Blustein describes three main reasons we work. We work to survive. That way, we can buy stuff to pay for our basic needs like food, shelter, education and medical care. Secondly, we work for social connection as it brings us into a broader social context. Our relationships with the people around us, such as work colleagues or clients, make us feel like we have our "place in the world." Finally, Self-Determination Theory maintains that we inherently want to grow as human beings and need self-actualisation and validation.

That sense of purpose came along with a need to be remembered. Life without memory was nothing but a succession of terror and tragedy. Humans resolved this problem by developing religious and cultural systems to make life worth living and derive pleasure from it.

As well as providing meaning, culture also gives us a way to be valued. A perverse effect is that we can revere some professions more than others. There is a perception that the so-called 'caring' professions, doctors, nurses and teaching, for example, are somehow more "worthy" than other more menial or venal type roles.

We create a hierarchy of job values that is bogus. The effect is to deny people meaningful jobs because they are in the wrong job. They are not; almost any job can have meaning and add value; it's just a frame of mind.

There has also been a prevailing belief, probably a legacy of the industrial revolution, that work should be hard. We have to work to earn time off to do the things we like. I know of some bricklayers who will do their minimum allotted hard work from early morning to early afternoon and then refuse any overtime because they want to go off and play golf. They are the exception to the rule because many of us draw a distinct line between work and play, and the two never mix. And that is fine.

We have voices inside screaming something like Monty Python's Lumberjack Song because we want to see ourselves leaping from tree to tree, finding our true selves and being free. Believe me—it's in there. Deep down, I've always known what I wanted to do. But I've never allowed myself to do it. I made excuses; I looked enviously at the people who had made it. I believed I've drifted through most of my life. I used to feel guilty about that, but I realise that I've gone through life, picking up experiences here and there, which has lead to the hot mess or cultural melting pot that is me today.

We think small

The bullshit they told you when you were young is still messing with you. I grew up in a culture where standing out was discouraged. It might have been the 1960s, but it wasn't all bell bottoms, flower power and the spirit of freedom; on the contrary. The wider society was still highly intolerant. The Summer of Love in 1967 was also a time when it was perfectly fine to go out on a Saturday night and give your wife a good slap because you were unhappy something hadn't been put back in the right place in the kitchen draw.

Society was still highly structured and stepping out of line was frowned upon. How often were we told not to "get ideas above our station?" A comedy sketch made famous by Ronnie Corbett, Ronnie Barker and John Cleese in 1966 about the class system with the smallest, working class Ronnie Corbett saying only "I know my place", was on TV a lot. It was part of the national psyche and a perfect illustration of why social mobility was (and remains) largely an illusion.

Expressions like "don't get your hopes up, so as not to be disappointed" - the motto of the permanently underachieving- were commonplace. "No one likes a show-off" was the ultimate slap for anyone trying to stand out. Although the counterculture of the late 60s contributed to loosening things up, there's no doubt that society was very top-down and space for individual thought was limited. The British are still obsessed with class, and we give credence to people because they speak with a posh accent.

The school system suited no one who didn't fit well with the industrial model. It was designed in the nineteenth century to produce fodder for the factories and the offices that managed them. It's built on a top-down compliance model like the military. Except there are no parade drills, press-ups and the risk of death if you step out of line on the battlefield. It's a system where anyone who asks questions, doesn't want to do things "in that order," or is creative in any way is pushed to one side. Sir Ken Robinson delivered what is still the most watched TED talk of all time in 2006 about how schools kill creativity and made some proposals to correct that. It doesn't look like he'll be heard anytime soon.

We think creativity is for artists-painters, musicians and writers. That way, it can be kept in a little box and under control. Sure, creativity is a great thing; we all admire it. But creatives are told to go and be creative somewhere else where it doesn't disrupt "normal" life.

Mainly working class, but also middle-class, people knew not to step out of line because there would be all hell to pay if they did. It's still the case. Even this weekend, as I write this, a Lord of the realm is being rightly slaughtered for complaining about the East London accent of a (black, female) TV presenter.

We've all sat down and thought about our place in the world at some point or other. And we've all been intimidated by the condescending views of other people. But it's a state of mind.

We grow up believing these things. Our parents and teachers say them because they mean well, but they do us no good. They teach us to know our place, be modest, and comply. Yet, the business owners that succeed don't comply. They get out of their lane, and I have ideas above their station, they stick their heads over the parapet and breathe the fresh air.

You don't need to be interesting all the time

Search "I have nothing interesting to say," and you will find articles about social anxiety, going to parties or meetings, and people finding themselves tongue-tied. If you're shy or introverted in any way, this can be a nightmare.

People often look at the extroverts in the room and think they have to be like them. So they believe they have to be "interesting" and "entertaining" to build any relationship. Like first date anxiety, they have to "win over" the person they are talking to.

That generally doesn't work in those kinds of situations. Dale Carnegie's advice from 80 years ago still stands, "be interested, not interesting." People like it when you ask them about them; it allows them to talk about themselves and removes the pressure of taking the lead.

There is an element of truth in this when it comes to telling our stories for marketing. We see our stories as our everyday life experiences to us, and we see them as bland. Add to this the baggage of what we were told when we were younger, and we build it up into a conviction that makes "I am not all that interesting."

I spent years thinking I'd drifted through life doing nothing remarkable. It was the safe option. Then I started talking to people with entirely different life experiences to me, and, oh what a surprise, they were interested like they'll be interested in yours.

Chapter 2

The Stories We Tell Ourselves When We're Young

We are mostly the product of our childhoods

I almost killed both my parents. Or so I thought. The guilt that came with that crippled me for years.

As if the things other people tell us weren't enough, our experiences—especially the early ones—also tell us stories that are often almost impossible to dislodge and stick around for our entire lives if we do nothing about them.

Even in a warm and loving upbringing, we can be relied on at some stage to sustain some form of psychological injury—the technical term is a primal wound.

Homo sapiens are unique among all living beings in that we have an inordinately long period of nurturing and apprenticeship before we're unleashed into the world to fend for ourselves. A foal will stand up 30 minutes after being born, a blue whale is sexually mature and a fully functioning adult by age five and the turquoise killifish in Mozambique is mature in 14 days.

Although it hasn't always been like that, human children

need almost two decades to be classed as adults. We can't walk until we are at least a year old and can rarely converse with any actual sense before age 2. By the time we reach 18, we will have spent 25,000 hours with our parents.

In the meantime, we are subject to the influence of home, our parents and the outside world. We remember the textures, the moods of the people around us and the tastes and smells of things important to us.

Our brains are more complex and advanced, so we take much longer to develop than other animals. We are physically vulnerable from having to be dressed, helped across the road, or requiring assistance to write our names. We are also emotionally vulnerable. We have difficulty working out where our feelings come from, how to interpret our parents' emotions from one day to the next and how to react when they say things to us. We take what adults say at face value and have little understanding of nuance or when things are expressed in the heat of the moment.

These are fertile breeding grounds for things to go wrong, even in the happiest households. Anything that happens doesn't need to be catastrophic. Often, the banalest of things or anodyne words can trigger a chain of misinterpretation and misunderstanding that lasts well into adulthood. I'm a long way from being an expert, so this is not a book about child psychology; the experiences of our early years almost always drive the stories we tell ourselves as adults. And we also think the things we experience when we are young leave hard-wired traces into our subconscious, never to be changed. That's not true.

Decades of research have revealed that the firstborn tend to be high achievers, the "good" kids and the ones who follow the rules. They're also more likely to be affected by anxiety and be self-critical. They'll bear the brunt of parental protectiveness, expectation and, in some cases, hopes and dreams. Yep, that sounds pretty much like me.

Whether it's not being able to deal with criticism, neglect or a feeling of being under-appreciated, childhood is just the gift that keeps on giving.

The climate in which we grow up at home affects us. A study by the University of Delaware in 2014 showed that the emotional support a child receives in the first three and a half years affects education, social life and romantic relationships even 20 or 30 years later.

Our childhoods make it challenging to move forward in a straight line—too timid or too assertive, too rigid or too accommodating. The Goldilocks Zone, where things are just right, is often difficult to reach.

We assume these imbalances are a permanent state. As adults, we tell ourselves things like, "I don't have any self-discipline"; "I'm no good with money", "I always end up in bad relationships", and so many others. Whilst these things may be true in the short term, there is no reason we can't correct them in adulthood.

Singular events can lead us to generalise about similar situations. The spectacle of a parent struggling with money can make us presume everyone has problems with money. Seeing one parent thwarted in their business ambition means that everyone struggles in their business. And so on and so on. So the stories we have to tell in later life are strongly influenced by what we experience in our early years.

Almost killing both my parents, but no ...

Of course, I came nowhere near finishing them off. I was born at home and my mother retained her placenta. I spent the second two weeks of my life in hospital. That's serious now, but it was often fatal in 1958.

Then my father contracted encephalitis by picking up measles from an unvaccinated me. He spent two months in hospital with a swelling brain and nearly died. The vaccine was only available a few years later.

They were undoubtedly severe problems but in no way my fault. They both survived and lived into their 80s, but the guilt I picked up on the way stayed with me for more than 50 years.

I don't have one of those "I survived a terrible childhood, and now I'm better" tales to tell. But the stories we tell ourselves form our attitudes for the future. And that's the thing.

I grew up knowing that my mother had been seriously ill when I was born, but I never understood why. We never talked about it at home except in the vaguest of terms in that oh-so-typically English way. I think you'd call it "in hushed tones." So for lack of information, I blamed myself.

I told myself that everything that went wrong was my fault. I used to say guilt was my middle name. And the best way to avoid things going wrong was to do nothing. I couldn't commit to anything real, however much I'd love to—I wouldn't be disappointed that way.

My father got ill just at the wrong time in 1963. He was in hospital for two months. In those days, the only way children got to see the inside of a hospital was as a patient. I was devastated and did not understand why my daddy had left me. I had to spend most of the day—or so it seemed to me-in this horrible place called school.

Playgroups and preschool activities didn't exist for me; I was thrown in at the deep end. My abiding memory of my first years at school was looking out of one of those windows reinforced with wire mesh because I'd been thrown out of the classroom because I was too upset to do anything.

Self-doubt crippled me. I was naturally shy through school and didn't dare push the boundaries as a young adult. I always felt something was missing. I couldn't bear to be wrong.

My guilt complex and inability to fess up stopped me from achieving my goals because I was too afraid to ask for things. Too scared of rejection. So I went into a shell for many years.

Let's not get dramatic though. My childhood was, like most others, a pleasant middle-class affair. There was no terrible abuse or hardship; we always had enough food, and the family was supportive.

I remember seeing the Bond film You Only Live Twice at the cinema on my ninth birthday—I still have the photograph of the friends who went with me.

Or hearing The Beatles' She Loves You on the radio when it came out and my mother lamenting that they were so lovely and clean-cut when they started as she saw them perform Let It Be in 1970.

I spent my summers in the park and fell in love with a 9-year-old Elaine Lewis when I was 11. We dated on the slides. It lasted two weeks, but I fell hard when it was over.

My first visit to the cinema was in Dublin. We went to Dun Laoghaire a couple of times, and the weather was always miserable. There must have been another film, but all I remember is Pinky and Perky.

The roads were much clearer in those days, you had the odd car parked up and down the road, and the rag-and-bone man could get up the street in his horse and cart without hitting anyone or anything. I remember he seemed ancient to me at the time. He probably hadn't reached his 60s; it just seemed like it. If he had, he would have been born in the nineteenth century. Even now, that blows my mind.

I was terrified of the compressed air units used to power pneumatic drills; I thought they could explode as I walked past. There's a video on YouTube of a group of men digging up the road opposite my local station in the early 1960s. They had no protective head gear and wore Wellington boots; that's how they rolled in those days.

Like many people, we didn't have a telephone at home. Our connection with the outside world was a phone box round the corner in Field End Road. It seems inconceivable these days that people could be that cut off from the world, but it wasn't until I was well into my teens that we were "on the phone." We had a colour TV before we had a phone. My grandfather never had one, and it's still a mystery how we communicated. Only when my father had a heart attack in 1974 and my mother had to get a neighbour to call an ambulance did we get one of our own.

I fell in love when I was 14 and never really recovered. More of that later. So yes, a pretty good childhood. Just a few screw-ups. The most common reason people think they have nothing to say is that they believe their lives are "normal" They can't imagine anything banaler than their experience. Others see things differently.

What we think our parents said

Despite what she might think, Jo Howarth is one of the best-functioning adults I know. Yes, she is perfectly capable of locking herself out of her own house, making her teenage children thoroughly ashamed of her (that's what parents are supposed to do, isn't it?) and collapsing into fits of laughter at the silliest of things. But there's much more to her than that.

She's very candid about her story because it informs the work she does today. Since training and practising as a hypnotherapist, she's sent the last decade or so using the experience of her early years to help large and small businesses and individuals face the challenges of their lives.

The Happiness Club has corporate programs and a network of trainers all on hand to help people through the everyday pressures of life and the bigger things that come up that need more work.

Growing up, though, she was confused. She was five years old when her parents separated. Even though she has no recollection of it, it proved to be one of the defining moment in her life. As they said in those days in the late 70s, her father "had an affair and ran away with another woman." As he "ran away from his family", he was portrayed as the evil man of evil men. There was no coming back from that.

Of course, the reality was more nuanced; Jo says he wasn't happy in his marriage and simply fell in love with somebody else. That somebody else had been his university sweetheart, and he couldn't resist. They met a few years later, and the rest is history, as they say. I can relate to that.

But you don't understand those things as a child. You see them in black and white. Especially when you think your father can do no wrong. Jo didn't understand why the people around her reviled this man she adored so much.

He was a vet and earned good money, but the salary went with him when he left. Her mother had been a nurse previously but hated it. So she resented enormously having to return to work to pay the bills. Her split loyalties meant that Jo picked up that it was her fault. She's very generous about it now, trying to understand how much she was hurting, but it's a situation likely to confuse any 5-year-old.

Eventually, her mother returned to the love of her life as well, although things didn't go too well with that relationship.

Her new stepfather "... had a miserable marriage. He'd been in the Navy and was an alcoholic. He didn't rage, but he was mean. He was very insecure and not happy. His main aim was to put everybody and anything else down as much as possible. He needed to assert his authority, his place. There wasn't any physical abuse, no big dramatic gestures, but just that underlying walking on eggshells feeling for fear of saying or doing the wrong thing."

On the outside, she had a happy middle-class upbringing. But that didn't stop her from feeling a fraud, especially when she won a bursary to go to a private secondary school. She felt she differed from her friends because she carried a perceived big secret that she was not the same as them. Their lives were probably far from perfect, but she thought she had something she couldn't reveal for fear of ridicule.

In reality, the local Somerset daughters of wealthy farmers suffered far more than her. Many had kept the local brogue and came across as not very sophisticated. Jo spoke—as she does now—perfect middle-England English and probably pulled it off much better than she imagined. She remained one of the crowd despite what she thought. Prejudice was alive and well and flourishing in the teenage offspring of the wealthy.

She had a diminished sense of self because she didn't know where she stood in the affection hierarchy. Parents weren't in the habit of telling their kids how much they loved them then. And, even though she knows now that her parents did, she grew up feeling they didn't. She only has memories of being told what she was doing wrong, how silly she was and feeling unloved. She was constantly on edge because she didn't know what to expect.

Jo grew up as a warm, empathic human being with a thriving business. She now knows she was experiencing anxiety, but at the time, she had great trouble working out where she stood in the bigger scheme of things. Minding her step at every corner for much of the time at home, torn between a father she adored and her mother she also loved, but who seemed to infer that having to go back to work was his fault, so Jo should hate him too.

At that age, in fact, at most ages, we never let the truth get in the way of a good story. She took many of those beliefs into adulthood running from crisis to crisis using whichever coping method she could. Until one day when she was well into her 30s after one stand up row with an unreasonable boss when she realised she had the power to change. The rest, as they say, is history.

A sense of belonging, but not there, elsewhere

Ash Ambirge never thought she belonged in that trailer park north of Philadelphia. She ended up there due to an unfortunate chain of events. Her destiny was elsewhere. She knew she was different.

Her birth father had said, "I can't do this", three days before she was born, and never wanted anything to do with her. He had another family to take care of that he'd forgotten to tell her mother about and didn't want the burden of a new child. Her mother had divorced her husband of ten years by then, but they'd stayed close friends. He did what close friends do and came over daily to help with the baby. He was the man Ash grew up with and considered her father even though the romantic relationship with her mother was not resumed.

She felt like a fish out of water. She'd grown up in a family of hardcore Democrats and progressive people who were "young and cool", but her stand-in stepfather developed a taste for fishing and wanted to find a place out of the city to do it. So they followed him to live in an apartment he provided for them in small-town America up North, where everyone was conservative, and no one had big ambitions.

They ended up in the trailer when her mother couldn't afford the rent on the apartment her stepfather had provided anymore. Nevertheless, Ash did everything with her stepfather-fishing in oversized waders, running to change dollars for quarters for the arcade he ran; she was in her element. But she hated the trailer.

Despite feeling out of place, she was among the most popular girls in school. As she had a big circle of friends and they invited her everywhere. That made her even more conscious of her difference, "... all of the other 15-year-olds had basements underneath their houses. We had wheels." So she'd do everything she could to ensure no one knew where she lived. When other kids' parents wanted to take her home, she'd tell them to drop her a few blocks away because she needed to pick up shopping from the corner store. She'd get dropped anywhere but not to that home.

But Ash is an independent woman and does not let things get in the way of what she wants to do. It didn't stop her from taking a degree in Spanish and public relations and a Masters' degree in linguistics, both subjects that seemingly had no practical uses until you realise what she does now.

But by the time she'd finished that degree, life had taken over and changed her forever.

She already had to grow up and juggle playing the big girl and enjoying her early years when she was younger than most. Her mother's anxiety was so bad she hardly ever went outside the house. In the earlier years, when she wasn't at home, she was with her stepfather. "He took me to Philly a few times a year to visit his old friends. They had huge, fancy houses, and it occurred to me that while he did not have houses like these, his personality was a secret weapon: people loved him. He took me fishing on all the rivers and put waders on me that were 10x too big. He enrolled me in fishing camps and tried to get me into his passion. He bought a small piece of land a few miles away and started inviting friends from the city to come camping. We went deer spotting every night in the summer and had contests to see who could spot the most. He honked the car horn under every bridge we went under. He was my hero. He was the antithesis to my mom's anxiety."

"One summer afternoon in 1998, when I was 14, he called me to come take the ride over the local hospital. The ride was through the woods and a bunch of meadows and fields, about 30 minutes away. He was there forever. When he came out, he handed me the pamphlet: "Helping your family cope with terminal cancer." He died in February when I was in 8th grade. I gave the eulogy; my mom couldn't face the funeral."

Her mother started having trouble with her legs. Her arteries were blocked from years of smoking and not going out due to her anxiety. She was waiting for open heart surgery when Ash discovered her mother had died alone in the trailer from a gruff County coroner; she called after finding a note on her door just saying, "call me."

She told me the world of grown-ups asked her to be an adult, but no one thought about the kid screaming inside. It was a turning point, and she was all alone. She says, "but with one death comes many: your identity goes into a blender and your relationship to the world is forever changed. Things you thought were true suddenly weren't. The person who used to be? Not anymore."

Her birth father died two months after her mother. She only found out when she went looking for him. His kids didn't want to know her either.

Alone again, indeed. I was an executor for my parents when I was 55 and 62. Ash was 19. How do you recover from that?

She admits she could have gone either way. She could have gone back to the house on wheels and wallowed in self-pity. But instead, she finished her degree in linguistics and Spanish and went on to a career in corporate America where she learned sales and marketing. But she made a terrible employee and eventually left and over the next ten years, she built a multi-million dollar copywriter business to prove it.

Despite her mother nipping her wannabe career as an anthropologist in the bud, Ash didn't have anyone around to instil self-limiting beliefs. There was no one to say, "don't get your hopes up," "don't stand out", or "be the same as everyone else." She thinks having no one to transfer their fears onto her has always been one of her most significant advantages. She turned a start in life that would have floored many of us into a springboard. She found the place where she belonged and her voice without restriction.

The business she built, The Middle Finger Project, was proof you could work differently, on your terms and answer to no one. That freedom eventually became a millstone, but that story is for later.

No one messes with Claire Russell

Like Ash, Claire Russell fitted a lot into her first 20 years. By the time she was 19, she'd almost died ... twice. Then she built and sold two businesses as a young woman in the predominantly white, male and middle-aged insurance industry and had a nervous breakdown before age 40. So where the hell do I start?

She woke up one morning when she was 13 with excruciating pain in her hip and collapsed on the floor. Her parents took her to the doctor who couldn't find anything wrong and even said she was faking to get out of school. So, he sent her home.

But she got worse. Her parents took her to hospital when she started getting delirious. It was just as well they did because the doctor who diagnosed her with septicaemia said she was within an hour of death.

Her hip was entirely shot and the orthopaedic surgeon she saw wanted to fuse it as she was too young to have it replaced. That would mean she'd never sit straight or walk properly again.

She wasn't having any of it as she knew she would, in effect, be disabled for the rest of her life. If there were a way to avoid that, she would find it. She held out against everyone—her parents included—and started to look for a surgeon who would agree to operate.

Two years and a good deal of pain later, she found one. He agreed to do the operation but on two conditions; she waited until she was 18 to sign the consent papers in her own right and saw someone who had already had the fusion procedure.

Claire and her parents met the girl and her parents at the surgeon's house for Sunday lunch. That was surreal enough, but she saw the young girl come in dragging her leg, and the first thing she said was, "don't fucking do it, worse decision I ever made." That solved the problem.

In reality, agreeing to the meeting was just for show. Claire was going ahead with the replacement whatever anyone said, but even her parents were convinced then.

She had the operation, and it went exceptionally well. She was up and walking within hours and hasn't had a problem with it since.

Indeed, she started going to the gym as part of her rehabilitation, that kicked off a life-long love of exercise.

If that wasn't enough, within a few months, she was out for Sunday lunch with friends when she was overcome with a strange feeling, "I felt like someone had poured a bucket of iced water over my head." Then she said to her friend, "I think I'm having a stroke", and lost consciousness. She was right; she was 19, had a stroke, and fell into a coma.

The doctor told her parents that she probably wouldn't survive, and if she did, she'd be in a vegetative state. But to everyone's surprise, after four weeks, she came around. She'd lost the right-hand side of her body and could hardly speak.

Claire says she has a superpower. She heals very quickly. She was up and moving in no time after her hip operation and determined that a stroke wouldn't stop her.

Perhaps with tongue firmly planted in her cheek, she told me that if ever she was in a superhero movie, she could have her head blown off and grow it back. I think she meant it.

Claire recovered her speech quickly and underwent physiotherapy to recover her motor functions, including learning how to grip a pen again. You wouldn't know today that it had ever happened.

She never recovered the sensation or spatial awareness on

her right side. I was at a party with her once in London when she managed to throw an entire glass of red wine over someone. She had the glass in her hand but couldn't feel it because she was in a conversation, gesticulating. Her lack of spatial awareness also means she constantly walks into walls and doors. But, as she says, that's a small price to pay. And she thinks it's pretty funny.

The experience also gave her an acute sense of self and determined her to do things according to her rules. It was excellent training for the rest of her life and the business she would set up when she was 23.

We're very good at burying emotional wounds

Whether it's not being able to deal with criticism, neglect or a feeling of being under-appreciated, childhood can be a fertile ground for developing hang-ups and problems we can hang onto well into adulthood.

What we experience in our early years strongly influences the stories we tell ourselves. I carried my lack of self-worth and guilt around for the best part of 50 years. Jo freely admits to destructive behaviours until she found her life's vocation. And Claire would probably not be as determined as she is if she had not suffered so much adversity in her teenage years.

These are our stories just as much as the things we want to shout about later in life. The timelines of our personal histories often hide many realities, good and bad. They are also some of the building blocks of our lives and, therefore, our businesses. The stories we tell ourselves are just as accurate as the things we experience and consider formative.

Chapter 3

But These Are The Stories Make Us As Business Owners

What did you want to do when you grew up?

My father dashed my hopes of being a train driver when I was 9. He told me that by the time I was old enough to drive a train, they wouldn't need drivers anymore.

So did you know what you want to do when you grew up? In a world where jobs and careers are far more transient than they used to be, having a single career is less important than it was. We are slowly moving towards a post-industrial employment model where it is no longer necessary or desirable to stay in the same job for an entire lifetime. We no longer need to take a train or drive a car to a place of work and add two hours and often more to the day to make someone else rich. It is even no longer necessary to stick to one single job when you can have two.

Some people have to work two or three jobs just to earn a living, and that's another type of nightmare entirely, but we are entering a new world of self-determined employment where the possibilities are boundless.

You don't need to know what you'll do when you grow up anymore. There's every chance that your view will charge more than once over a lifetime. But some people just knew. They had positive experiences when they were young that made them who they are today. Amy was an entertainer, Fabi was made to run a successful online business, and Emma just wanted to help people. Let me tell you about them.

Amy was always going to be a storyteller

Amy Harrison grew up in a family of natural storytellers. She was hard-wired for creativity at an early age. Growing up in East Yorkshire with older siblings and a family of raconteurs, she says she had to have sharp elbows to get heard. The family were harsh critics, so they'd let you know the minute you were boring. To get noticed, she had to be good.

She successfully auditioned for a band singing Free's All Right Now when she was just 11. I'd have loved to have been a fly on that wall because that song requires some gusto. The group was still performing together when she was 17. She also sang in a gospel choir when she was 15 or 16. She loved seeing the faces of the audience change when, despite any nerves she might have had when starting when they heard what she describes as her "booming and gospely" voice, they realised she had the chops.

There was no plan. She'd try something, discovered she enjoyed it and got a good response. Rinse and repeat. That sounds like an excellent way to do things.

She sometimes had a rough time as a small redhead in senior school, not with the people who knew her but with others around her. She says if we ever have to deal with a vicious dictator in the future, there's little point in applying sanctions. Adolescents can be very creative in their cruelty. Thirty minutes in the back of the school bus with a group of 13- and 14-year-olds will do the trick-the most straightforward and cheapest way to beat an adversary into submission.

She surrounded herself with stories throughout her childhood and adolescence, especially when the mean creativity of the kids around her kicked in. She says she escaped to an imaginary plane in her head and spent a lot of time daydreaming. Only later, when she started connecting the dots, did she realise the importance of doing this. It helped immensely with visualisation and having ideas for stories, so when she started to get paid for them, she was ready to go.

Her grades didn't suffer despite all that. She was academically gifted and seemingly Oxbridge-bound. Still, a misunderstanding over exams and a handbrake turn led her to Bournemouth for a degree in scriptwriting for film and television. Her teachers were dismayed, but the move would later form the basis of her entire writing career.

She worked in a call centre in Canada and would have stayed had she been able to find a job to sustain her. It was there she picked up communication skills that would no doubt serve her later. Her writing career finally kicked off when she was sitting at her desk in an office in Brighton daydreaming again and noticed some pigeons "scratching around in the shit and dirt and being envious of their freedom." They were having more fun than her.

She started writing content for pennies but loved it. Then she joined a bluegrass band because music and Amy will never be very far apart. She thought she was winning at life, writing for a living, singing for fun. She had complete freedom over what she could and couldn't do. Her core value was and still is, "Is it fun?"

I first discovered her doing some quirky videos illustrating copywriting points. She'd looked around and saw how other people were doing and realised there were gaps she could fill with her skills, make a difference, and earn a lot more. Amy had no truck with the boring talking head, "you have to know your ideal client" snooze fest. She dressed up and role-played to make her points in a way I've seen no other copywriter do. All that showtime stuff when she was a teenager was starting to pay off.

She pitched to some prominent people. She got to guest post on Copyblogger, still one of the biggest copywriting websites in the world. She set up a heavily optimised landing page so that a famous marketer would notice her. Her entertainment background has given her the confidence to make videos to send to potential clients rather than a boring email pitch.

Amy is an entertainer at heart; she's been doing it since she was young. Whether a singer in the band or a writer for large brands worldwide, she's still telling stories in her work and doing what she was always meant to do. Oh, and she married the banjo player in the bluegrass band.

The things that make you independent

Fabi Paolini was born to be independent, and it's no surprise that she's built not one but two internet marketing businesses in two different languages and two different cultures. She was born international.

Born in Brazil, her father was in the oil industry and, as a result, got to work around the world. She spent much of her childhood on the move between Venezuela and Spain. She had several stints in the US and even a stay in India. She had quite a time in her formative years.

Living in the US near Roswell, famous for its fake aliens, she was immersed in an English-speaking world and school outside the house. She learnt to speak English when she was seven but was not allowed to speak it at home to enable her to maintain her Spanish. Children of that age are learning sponges, and she was bilingual within two months.

She feels lucky to have maintained both cultures because she's known people who spoke English at home too and lost contact with their mother tongue as a consequence.

It's served her well beyond the advantages of bilingualism. She realised that if she could learn a language in two months, she could do anything. She's self-reliant and determined and has a work ethic and ability to get to the point that would be the envy of many.

Living in Miami helps her juggle her two languages and two cultures. She attended American schools when she was back in Venezuela, so she spoke English all the time. In high school, most of the students were Venezuelan, and everyone used a form of Spanglish, a hybrid language developed naturally that only the students could understand.

That reminds me of my time in an English-speaking community in Paris, where a kind of Franglais developed in the same way. It's natural when you have two languages swimming around in your brain. When you can't think of a word in one language, it comes out in the other.

Mixing two languages is apparently a sign of being truly bilingual. She went to a purely Venezuelan high school to qualify for University and only spoke Spanish there. Reverting to a monocultural environment was a shock because she could no longer use her previous Lingua Franca. But Fabi being Fabi, she adapted just fine.

However, moving from an Americanised system to a Venezuelan one imposed cultural shifts even on her. And as events developed, it was decided that rather than go to a Venezuelan university, she'd go to the University of Miami.

She says that despite growing up in different countries; she was and still is very Venezuelan. She had to stay rooted in her identity, she would have had problems otherwise. Moving around was, in fact, the source of her strength. She's not a rebel. She was the good kid at school, always had good friends, got good grades and loved studying-because of that independent spirit. It's rare to meet someone who is genuinely not bothered by what people think of her and does not use that as an excuse to be a douchebag.

When she graduated, she went to work for the advertising agency Leo Burnett, first in Miami and then in Venezuela that she always considered her long-term home. But advertising wasn't what she hoped it would be, and she was soon working for herself.

"... I don't have a normal path, I'm the main breadwinner, my family, my husband works for me. And it's something that I could be very well (...) judged by many people from my (Hispanic) culture, my community, my family. But that's not my problem. That's your problem. If you don't like it, deal with it. This is how I live my life."

Things were going well in Venezuela. Fabi had done an MBA because she was interested in helping businesses grow.

So, when she went to the US for the birth of her first daughter, the intention was always to go back.

"We had a work visa in the US. My husband was working here and promoting here and doing things here. But my plan was to give birth and come back. I have an apartment in Venezuela with a baby nursery with a closet full of clothes, with food in the pantry with everything that I haven't touched in six years is still there."

She gave birth in September, intending to go back in November. As the situation deteriorated at home and as the family was coming for Christmas, they postponed it to the New Year. By March, she and her husband realised the universe might be telling her she should stay. She'd moved around enough. It was time to drop anchor. The problem was that with no way of exporting her Venezuelan business to Miami, she'd have to start again.

She needed money to live, so she thought with her feet. She calculated she needed $5,000 a month to live in Miami, but she was charging $500 per website for her clients. She would need ten a month to survive. Every month. And she forgot to factor in taxes.

That wasn't sustainable, so she decided on a radical solution. She raised her prices to $5000, tenfold. That's what "I can do anything" confidence and the story you tell yourself can do for you.

Looking back, she wonders if she wasn't crazy (maybe she was). It was perhaps her background and her "what the hell" attitude, but at the time, it seemed normal.

Besides raising her prices tenfold, she was interested in more than just websites, but in how business, particularly Internet business, worked. Never one to lack confidence, she developed coaching through difficult times, working out how things worked, getting into debt just to live but making money nevertheless. She developed her messaging little by little, and things got better. And it worked.

Her life now centres around her business and her family.

She says she and her husband are a partnership. She's forged a lifestyle and a routine that works for them.

Her daughters are used to her working and generally don't interrupt (often). She says it's good for them to have a role model.

She is hyper-productive and finishes everything she needs to do between 10 and 3. She's built a successful multiple 6-figure business and-more importantly-a life that works for her. And she has no plans to move home again. Miami suits her very well.

Fabi probably didn't think "when I grow up, I want to be a business owner" when she was young. But all her life experiences, travelling abroad, learning on the fly and having to deal with new situations quickly made her wholly unsuited to being an employee. She is in her element.

Emma didn't have the greatest of starts in life

There's no other way to describe it, really. Emma grew up in an emotionally abusive home, but she has used that experience as a driver for her business and her mission to do some good in the world.

She had an older brother and sister who she didn't grow up with; her brother was kicked out of home before she was born. Her sister followed when Emma was three. Up to that point, she'd been Emma's primary caregiver. Her father left when she was six, and from that point, she had a lot of responsibility pushed on her. She was herself kicked out at 16, leaving only her younger brother at home.

She was confused. There was only one person left to trust, herself. Emma was homeless, with just two boxes of schoolwork and a few clothes to her name. She'd lost everything precious to her. Probably because she'd had to grow up quickly from a young age and had developed a strong sense of self and didn't get involved in drugs and crime like many in her situation.

Between the ages of 16 and 21, she moved 16 times. Ultimately, she'd had enough of the uncertainty and bought herself a house as an anchor.

Like most people in Norwich, she worked at financial conglomerate Norwich Union (now Aviva) for a while before doing the rounds of the different firms of Financial Advisers. She hated it. In retrospect, she was just biding her time before finding her calling.

After ten years in finance, she found a job as an outreach worker with a non-profit organisation supporting women. This time, she loved it. She'd fallen into her vocation. She learned British Sign Language and launched headfirst into becoming a trained coach. After two years, the non-profit ran out of funds and was left with a choice. Either go back to financial services and hope the funding came or follow her dream. There was only ever going to be one winner of that competition—she travelled the world for a year.

When she returned, she started an Open University degree in Combined Social Sciences and Criminology. At the same time as working full-time supporting someone with an acquired brain injury she worked part-time in the probation service. It was a turning point and validation. It would be six years before she graduated. That day was one of the proudest of her life.

She also founded a social enterprise as a lived experience leader, using her professional training and background to work with people who couldn't afford her regular coaching rates— especially young people and survivors of domestic abuse. She helps them steer away from the pain of their pasts toward fulfilling their own lives.

Once she decided to start a business, there was no turning back. She bought her domain name on the spot and took things from there.

She's undergone extensive professional and academic training and bases her work on the deep empathy and gentle strength she has learned through real-life experience. Her passion, drive and purpose come from wanting to support people in a way she didn't enjoy when she was younger. "I love coaching", she says, it's the only valid reason for running any kind of business, and I love seeing people be happy and successful."

"I want to help people like me. You don't need to have had loads of trauma or to feel worthy or good enough." She also works a lot with teenagers because those are people for whom she feels great empathy. "I love to think I can help teenagers and support them to change their future. How cool is that?"

Neely Khan: forged by her childhood

Neely Khan decided she would be a writer when she was eight. Many 8-year-olds have ideas like that and change them three or four times by the time they're 12. Not Neely; she achieved her dream by sticking to her guns. However, the road may have been a little rocky.

I've interviewed people from many cultural and intellectual backgrounds for this book. Many have lived in different countries and speak more languages than I do. Many have more varied cultural and intellectual backgrounds than me. Neely beats them all. When I asked her how many languages she speaks, she had to use her fingers to count them.

"It's the beauty of being South Asian", she says. As well as English, she speaks Hindi and Urdu. She counted these as one language because of their similarities but admitted they were more or less separate when pressed by me. She also speaks Gujarati. She also understands Arabic, Marathi, and several other—to be honest, I lost count. In her family, though, she's a little behind in the language league table; other members speak more than her.

Neely's childhood and much of what she learned during it made her. She learned resilience early, but she's used it as a driver in her business today. She was born to do one thing.

She was born in Leytonstone in the same hospital as David Beckham and is proud of that claim to fame. Ten years or so previously, her parents had arrived from Dar es Salaam on a quest to replicate the wholesale business her father had grown so they could build a better life. Her early life with her extended family in London was comfortable and happy. Her father set up a family-run business with his first cousin, and it was going well. "And in our family, your first cousins are like your siblings; they're as good as your brothers and sisters. Family relationships are hugely significant, and blood is thicker than water. So, when they went in business together, nobody thought anything of it; it's the thing you would just do.,"

While Neely, her siblings and her mother were away in Tanzania, her father got home one day to realise everything had gone. They'd been left penniless. It may be a sixth sense, but when she got back, she knew something was wrong as they walked in the door.

She was right; everything had changed. The family suddenly left the big house where they lived; Neely was torn away from her friends and activities and headed for a council estate in Birmingham. She was understandably angry and still bears some resentment towards the city even though she still lives there. She was determined to hate the place.

Her father's confidence was shot so much he never worked again. Her mother worked three jobs, mainly for the money, but Neely thinks she perhaps wanted to escape him. He was diagnosed with OCD before the business failed, which got worse as time passed. She found herself alone with him for long periods. She now wonders how she lived like that for so long, but it was the only thing she knew. For her, it was "normal" everyday life.

And that is how most of us live. Our personal experience is our only reference point, so we tend to think everyone lives like us. The fact that people don't is one of the things that make us extraordinary. She couldn't watch TV much until she was well into her teens, so she lost an entire tranche of popular culture. Perhaps due to her lived experience or nature, she was an introvert who liked reading and writing her stories.

I saw my father having a nervous breakdown when I was 15, but at the time, I thought he was just being a dick. Seeing what the experience did to her father was worse. She says that she recognises his depression through her adult eyes, but 7-year-old girls don't see that.

She told her father she wanted to be a writer when she was eight, right after a parents' evening. He was not just supportive; he was exceptionally so. But that was also the problem. He became obsessively supportive.

So, he made her read "an obscene number of books, out loud, with the expressions" and would get angry when she made mistakes. He set story writing challenges over the weekend with timed tasks where she had to develop a story.

She says, "this sounds like I had the worst childhood ever", and it would be hard to disagree. But, surprisingly, perhaps, she bears no resentment. Some of her best traits as an adult and business owner come from that childhood. She is a world champion taker of criticism and negative feedback; she has "ovaries of steel." It's given her inner strength and resilience to face the worst situations. When she goes into survival mode, she generally feels indestructible. She attributes much of that to her father.

There was, however, a reaction. Teenage Neely had a lot of pent-up anger over her parents and the world. She ran away from home and didn't contact her parents for two and a half years. Despite this, sensible Neely was never far away, as she managed to pass all her exams and get to Cambridge while staying with friends. She didn't see getting to Cambridge as a big deal; it was just the result of the discipline she'd learnt over the years. It was as though sensible Neely and wild child Neely were having one hell of a Battle Royale in her head.

Once she got to Cambridge, she was a model student during the day and a party girl in the evening. The student's life experience is something of a blur to her because she thinks she was either drunk or high most of the time. Then she got pregnant.

It was a one-night stand, and the brief conversation she had with the father afterwards told her she'd better get used to being a single mother. She'd only just got back in touch with her parents, so she avoided telling them until the last minute, two weeks before her due date. Her family is highly traditional, and there was some drama when she broke down and told her mother, but they've been supportive.

Neely told me being a mother changed her life. After her daughter was born in the hospital, she said she was the happiest girl alive. She kicked all her "bad habits" overnight and threw herself into motherhood. She even said she loved struggling with a pushchair on and off buses.

After many dead-end jobs and a failed attempt to make a go

of it with her daughter's father, she struck out on her own. She'd never stopped writing since she was a child; for her, it's physical. She finds therapy and healing by sitting down daily with a pen and paper. She even says she feels uneasy when she can't do it.

She's been going ten years or so now. There have been many ups and downs, feast and famine periods, but now she supports herself and her daughter, and she couldn't be happier. And she's just published a book. It happens to the best people!

We have choices now

What you wanted to be when you grew up is no yardstick to judge what you become. We all wanted to be train drivers, nurses, or any number of professions. I wanted to be an architect, but misplaced advice from a chemistry teacher about my Maths not being good enough put paid to that. Structural engineers do the calculations. History of Art would have been a good idea.

Our early experiences have a massive positive or negative influence on whom we become later. Claire Russell and Ash Ambirge used them as drivers, Jo Howarth and I took a bit longer to work things out. Neely and Amy just knew, and Emma and Fabi almost had greatness thrust upon them.

We live in more flexible times than when I grew up. Self-employment won't be an option in the school careers office anytime soon, but people increasingly see it as a possibility and not just a response to redundancy. People now see it as a way of continuing a profession without the hassle of looking for a new job. It's a viable choice for people who don't want the restrictions of being an employee and are looking to do things on their terms. Far more than the four women I've spoken about here, you can see it across the spectrum of professions. It's a great time to be alive.

I grew up in a world where you most definitely went to school, got good grades and a good job and greased the wheels of the system until you retired, so you could start to enjoy life, what you had left of it anyway. Maybe there's a way to combine work and life in a way that means we get enjoyment and fulfilment first—just a thought.

Chapter 4

Me? It Started With A Frozen Burger

There was never a plan to be self-employed

Except for my painter-decorator grandfather, whom I never knew because he died when I was six months old, no one in my family had ever been self-employed. My brother and I grew up in a culture where you went to school, got good grades and got a good job—and lived happily ever after. Our father only had one employer, British Rail, so why shouldn't we?

We're both in our sixties now and have been self-employed for more than half of our adult lives. How did we go from the accepted path of our teenage years to choosing to be independent in our adult years? Well, it certainly wasn't planned like that.

For most of my life, my significant decisions have been based on impulse rather than reason, and I made things up as I went along. I was also the first in my family to go to University, not because I wanted a better job, but because I fell in love with the idea of academia, and I wasn't going to give that up. I wanted to study History and carry on French for their intrinsic value, not because I thought they would get me anywhere.

I went to France because, at the time, it seemed the logical thing to do. I stayed because I fell in love with the place, not because of any career advantage. I returned to get a job but went back in purely personal circumstances and, in the process, wrecked a promising career.

I rolled with the punches. The downside was that I had the impression that life was something that happened to me rather than the other way around. I've drifted through life, picking things up along the way. The upside is that I've picked up experiences and cultures that I probably wouldn't have with a more linear path. I'm only now coming to realise the value of that. It's a trade-off, I guess, but now I've come to terms with it, it doesn't matter anymore.

I though I'd stay with History for life

In 1975, History smacked me in the face. First with the Industrial Revolution and the History of Building, and then the two Henry Tudors, Elizabethans and the English Civil War. I was never going to do anything else. I even questioned my love of French. You can have two loves, can't you?

When I got to University, the knowledge bug struck me even more. There was so much of it I didn't know where to turn and what to do first.

I spent hours in the modernist Basil Spence-designed library at the University of Sussex in my third year reading Edmund Burke and the only biography of Charles James Fox ever published. I was in my element, and if I could I would do it all over again. I can still smell it.

Ironically, perhaps, for an atheist, I became fascinated by

the mid-seventeenth-century millenarians who appeared in the aftermath of the English Civil War.

History tells the stories of real people. Not just kings and queens, wars and peace, economics and demographics; it's all about people who lived and breathed just like you and me. So many of their stories have been lost because there was no way to record them beyond the oral tradition. But now, our stories are more important than ever in this hyper-connected world.

I was happy in academia, doing a History degree and playing around with French. I wasn't ever going to leave if I could avoid it. I had a Masters', a PhD and a life in an ivory tower teaching seventeenth-century English History to discerning and interested grads and undergrads all planned out. I'd do research and write books, and by the time I got to the age I am now, I'd have carved out quite a name for myself. I didn't see a time when I wouldn't be in daily contact with History and teaching.

But I must have got stage fright when I got to the final exams. I flunked them on the back of an oral exam on the 1848 French Revolution, so don't talk to me about *Les Misérables!* Just like that, I didn't have the right grades to do the Masters'. Worse, I didn't pursue the matter because I thought that was the end of the road—there was nothing to be done. Maybe it was, maybe it wasn't, but I didn't have the self-belief to pursue the issue. It was much easier to cry over what might have been. And that was that. All of a sudden, it was gone.

The problem was that I had no Plan B either. Others did what they called the milk round and found jobs, employers, and grown-up stuff like that, and I had nothing.

So, why did I go to France?

"Calais Maritime, ici Calais Maritime, tous les voyageurs descendent de voiture."

I can hear it like it was yesterday. The announcement was the clarion call for the people travelling on the three-hour journey from Paris to Calais to get off the train and get on the boat that would take them back across the Channel.

As a child, it was a sign that the holiday was over and school was about to start again in the next few days.

I was good at French at school, as I had a head start on the other kids because I'd been enjoying adventures with Xavier and Georges in the advanced Nuffield language programme since I was 8. This was at a time when very few studied a foreign language in primary school. Perhaps being good at it was why I loved it so much.

I'd been made aware of the notion of foreign languages by the travelling I'd done with my parents. In Spain, my brother and I mixed with German and Danish kids in addition to the Spanish ones. Kids can speak different languages at that age and still get on.

It took me a while to understand what a foreign language is and how it works. I remember being perplexed about what the other kids were saying and thinking at least once, "well, they must think in English." I don't know what superpower I thought they had that I was missing. There must be a movie to be made about a superhero who thinks in one language but speaks another.

I spent so much time on trains and ferries until I was about 30 that France became a home from home very early on. I was used to travelling, used to the country; it wasn't foreign to me by the time I got there. I'd been primed for years.

By the time I got to degree level, I'd been suckered in and didn't want to give it up. Language and culture had become part of me.

I was ripe for becoming French, even before my break up with history. As soon as I got to my new office in Paris, I wanted to blend into this new identity.

I thought I spoke French

In the summer of 1980, I was 21 and cocksure I thought I spoke French. I was in the second year of a degree. I'd learned my subjunctive and my vocabulary had expanded to things real French people say rather than what textbooks think. I was ready for anything Paris could throw at me.

But I felt apprehensive on the plane. It wasn't my first time working in France, I'd picked pears a couple of years before. But now I was going to be in an office. I would have to rely on my intellectual talents rather than my physical ones.

I'd come with my father and brother, who worked for British Airways and got us cheap tickets. I think the old man just came along for the ride.

We got the plane and then the train into Paris and, this may be my memory playing tricks on me here, they left me at the station. Over 40 years later, I can't work out why.

I have to admit now to panicking slightly at being left alone. I was used to having others around me just in case something went wrong. I want to say I was plonked in Paris with nowhere to go, but I've no doubt my father wouldn't have let me go there- even at the age of 21 without booking at least one night in a hotel.

I remember walking down rue de Rivoli with a sense of wonder, taking it all in. This was Paris, the City of Light. I was in awe and probably already a little in love.

On a Sunday night at the end of June 1980, Rue de Rivoli was a magical place to be. If you stand in the middle of the street and look northwards, you can see an uninterrupted line to the Place de la Concorde and up the Champs Elysées to the Arc de Triomphe. The other way gives you a straight line to the Place de la Bastille.

There is always heavy traffic there in one of the most famous cities in the world. Cars and small trucks, taxis, and dark green-painted buses vying for attention and supremacy in the race to the end of the street at the Place de la Bastille. Parisians don't stop to take in the things that surround them. The traffic only slows for traffic lights strategically placed at intersections with other streets. It would be one hell of a drag racetrack otherwise.

I was trying to take it all in. The people, the buildings, the former royal residence at Les Tuileries, the Hôtel de Ville, the four buildings of La Samaritaine, the largest of those wonderfully nineteenth-century *"grands magasins"* still surviving today.

I was on the cusp of an adventure I did not know would change my life. It made me international, bilingual and multicultural and a complete person. But for the moment, once installed, my first concern was dinner.

In the days when the only fast-food outlets were Wimpy bars, self-styled "self-service" restaurants were littered all over Paris and major cities across France. That's where I discovered *"poulet aux pruneaux"*, I thought mixing fruit and meat was a very strange thing to do. Not for the first time, I was wrong. It's a classic and a staple of French family cuisine.

Self-service restaurants were overgrown staff canteens, really; they served a purpose for families looking for a cheap meal out or travellers passing through like me. They were basic, served beer and wine, and they suited 21-year-old me to a T. I may have had one beer too many, but at least I slept well.

I only remember a little about the journey on the metro to my first day at work in a Paris office. The leap into the unknown that meant walking through the door would normally have terrified me, but somehow I felt confident. It was almost as if I knew something.

I went to work for the first time in an office where they spoke a foreign language. I was starting a new life in a new country.

I stayed in a hotel for a week and then sublet a chambermaid's room on the 6th floor in the rue de la Convention near Montparnasse with no bathroom from someone in the office related to the family that owned the company that produces Boursin cheese.

Eventually, I learned what it was like to travel on those commuter trains I'd overtaken for years in fast trains on the run in from Spain in the 60s and 70s. I'd spend the weekends taking it all in, discovering places like Gilbert Jeune or the FNAC stores, the places to go for your fill of culture. I met real French people in actual work situations. My assimilation was almost complete.

The experience in Paris changed me forever. When I got to the British Rail/Sealink office that Monday morning, I met Mavis—obviously an excellent French name. She was a 50-something woman from Skipton in Yorkshire who had married a Frenchman and had been in Paris for years. She spoke a broad Yorkshire in English that she didn't bother to change when she spoke French. Much to her colleagues' amusement and sometimes incomprehension, French or otherwise. She was still in Paris in 2014, working as a storyteller. I'd love to be able to look her up.

Mavis was part of the furniture at BR. Like me, she had a fixed-term contract but returned every year because her husband, Chris, was the office manager. Born in France to British parents, Chris was one of the few people I have known with two mother tongues. She was as good a person as any to show me the ropes.

That Monday morning (1st July 1980), Mavis took an enormous maroon-coloured ring binder and explained the products I would be selling. Some I knew, like the Red and Green Rover bus passes and the cross-channel ferry services, but others, like Train + Hotel, were new to me.

I thought I was doing well; my university French was holding up. I'd grown up with trains and travelling on them. I had this covered.

The office in the Boulevard de la Madeleine had a big long counter, like an old-style airline, with two or three people dealing with public visitors and everyone else getting on with their jobs in an open office behind. I'd noticed a constant and slightly annoying pinging in the background while Mavis explained the products to me. I realised later it was the phone ringing. In hindsight, it probably wasn't a great advert for customer service because it made it seem like the phone was ringing all the time and no one was answering.

Other people who weren't employed to answer the phone walked around as if they did not have a care in the world. In reality, we were flat-out taking one call after another with very few breaks. That made the situation worse.

It was about 11 o'clock on my first day when Mavis told me to "answer the phone." I hadn't reckoned on that, somehow. I wasn't entirely sure what I would do in this new job, but I was convinced it didn't involve phones. Phones terrified me at the best of times in my native language, so being asked to answer in a foreign one sent my heart rate spiralling. What if I couldn't answer the questions? But it was one of those times when I couldn't say no. It was part of the job, after all.

So I answered the phone. I couldn't answer a lot of the questions at first. They were mainly from other travel agents who wanted to book the Calais-Dover hovercraft. It was hard. They initially shouted at me, but that mattered less because I couldn't understand what they were saying.

For two weeks, I was lost; I struggled to learn the specialist travel industry vocabulary. I struggled without all the gestures and context-free language that talking on the phone implies, but when I came out the other end, I was full-fat bilingual ... and bicultural.

The French I'd learned was academic; almost anyone would understand it, but it wasn't how real people spoke. It was a baptism of fire. In the first half of July 1980, I learnt how to contract words like the French. I learnt how to run words together—*t'as pas deux balles ? J'sais pas. t'es dingue ?*—I learnt the specialist travel industry vocabulary but above all, I learned to feel at home in a foreign language. I adopted the mannerisms and habits that have stayed with me for a lifetime.

Learning French and the public washroom

It was a bumpy ride. I wanted to be perfect out of the gate and avoid making mistakes. Mistakes were a source of great shame.

My sixth-floor chambermaid's room came with a wash basin down the hall but not a shower. I may have been a 21-year-old student in 1980, but I had standards. The big station at

Montparnasse had shower facilities, and it was on the way to work. So I would drop in several times a week to look clean and presentable.

Staff provided everything you could require to look wholesome when you left, towels, soap, shampoo, and the like. But I wanted a comb. The rather imposing lady in the public washroom threw me a withering "who the hell do you think you are?" type of look when I asked. It was only later that I realised that rather than asking for *"un peigne"*, I'd asked for a *"peignoir"*—a dressing gown. I'd have slapped myself too.

But you don't learn without making mistakes do you? Tell that to the 21-year-old me. I was mortified. My desire to assimilate was so intense I'd cringe every time I got something slightly wrong. I'd work out the meaning of words by the context in which people used them. In later years, this tactic would serve me well as a translator and a copywriter, but then, it was an avoidance strategy.

Somehow, it worked; I understood everything around me. I could watch TV and not be confused and, to my great surprise, I went to the cinema in 1981 to see François Truffaut's penultimate film *La Femme d'à Côté* with a young Fanny Ardent and Gérard Depardieu and understood everything. When I understood comedians, Coluche and Raymond Devos, Guy Bedos and all the others, I knew I'd arrived.

A year or two later, I had an argument on the phone in French with a woman who wanted to speak to a British person. "But, I am British", "No, I want to speak to a British person", "But I am." The discussion went on for a while in an absurd Monty Pythonesque way before she hung up on me. I took that as a compliment. I'd assimilated.

A square peg in a round hole

At some point in 1984, my boss told me I was a square peg in a round hole. It hurt at the time, but in my heart, I knew he was right.

I was working at the Franco-British Chamber of Commerce in Paris, answering the phone and finding manufacturers of weird and wonderful widgets in the backstreets of Grantham, Taunton, or Newcastle-under-Lyme. You can do that kind of search in five minutes these days without leaving the comfort of your desk. But then, it was dead-end and I hated every minute of it.

In the 1980s and into the early 1990s, I'd moved on from Sealink to the Franco-British Chamber of Commerce, back to Sealink and a three-year stint at British Rail in London before going Paris with American Express Travel. I realise now that I was never made to be an employee. I was still an academic at heart.

The 1980s didn't sit well with me. It was an age when success was measured by how much money you had. Business owners like Bernard Tapie were on prime-time TV in France, with all the rhetoric that came with them. The self-satisfied, "haven't I done well?" people I met through the Chamber of Commerce didn't help either. It felt plastic, just like the sound of the Dire Straits CDs that symbolised the era so much. There had to be something else.

I was a square peg in a round hole, not just in terms of my job but also culturally. I was an academic in the wrong world. Being in France probably softened the blow, they talk of the aggressiveness of the "Anglo-Saxon" world, but it wasn't a pleasant time to be alive for a sensitive soul like me. If you didn't fit in, you were told, "this is the way to be; otherwise, you're a loser," but I didn't want to be like that.

In reality, I was an intellectual unhappy in a work environment. I'd have been much better in a situation where I could sit and think and write. It took me a long time to get there.

I recently realised that I experienced rejection by academia as a breakup; I was heartbroken. I had to find a way back to it after it rejected me. I took it personally and continued to lick my wounds for many years afterwards. I had no idea where my place was. It certainly wasn't in this world. It felt like if you didn't fit into the system, you were essentially a bad person.

I was a terrible employee, not cut out for the rigours of office life. I remember leaving the office at American Express in Paris one winter's evening after a particularly stinky day. I walked down the steps to the metro, thinking there must be a better way of working and earning money. I dreamed of a world where I could do two or three things that were not necessarily related and get paid for them all.

I didn't realise that people had been doing that for years, but my schooling in the "get a job and stick with it" mentality was ingrained. I didn't know you could be anything else than a slave to the corporate machine.

The thought of living and working on my own scared the shit out of me in my early thirties. But losing a job, a relationship breakdown, and moving to the country forced my hand. How I got there is a long story, but here I am, 30 years later, and I wouldn't be anywhere else.

About that frozen burger

In 1996, I was sick of supermarket own-brand frozen beef burgers. Yes, they have them in France, too; it's not all gastronomy and fine wines you know. I'd been eating them with a concoction of kidney beans, a small tin of Buitoni bolognese sauce, and a dollop of quite fiery Harissa. In a burger bun. Don't knock it till you try it. I got much better with my cooking and eating habits later, but towards the end of 1996, I'd become depressed.

I listened to the radio, but not to music. I was living in a bedsit, seemingly cut off from the world. I'm trying to remember how I occupied my days. I find it incredible that I had all that time on my hands and didn't read anything. Depression creeps up on you without you being aware. I was drifting. Eventually, it came to a crunch.

I'd hit rock bottom after I narrowly failed the competitive exam they make you take if you want to train to be a teacher in France. I'd written essays in French on Shakespeare and Wilkie Collins and was mightily pleased with myself. I'd got through the written part, much to my surprise and those around me— including my mother. The oral part, however, was more tricky. It came with a task to present a grammatical breakdown of a sentence—the French love grammatical analysis. The noun and verb groups were fine, but I had nothing to say about the syntax. I failed to make the cut by 0.4%.

I sometimes shudder when I think of the prospect of teaching English to recalcitrant 13-year-olds who most definitely didn't want to be in a classroom with me. I doubt if I'd have lasted a year. I consider that a bullet dodged, though, because I and the highly hierarchical French education system would not have got on.

In the meantime, I'd got to the end of the road with the unemployment payments that had got me through my studies. I was now on subsistence money designed to cover (not even) the barest essentials. So what was next?

One of the perverse effects of depression is that it narrows your options because the walls of your self-belief close in on you. You see the world in your little circle, and new and exciting ideas just don't occur. Ideas can, however, be thrust in front of you.

I saw an ad in the local employment office for translators. Not the most conventional approach of attracting qualified professionals, but I knew nothing of that at the time.

I had a feeling that I could be good at it. My teacher training had sparked a liking for a discipline that I'd hated at university. So, as unqualified as I was, I decided I should go for it. After all, I spoke French and English—what could possibly go wrong?

I thought of Patrick Piers as a prospective employer, but he was, in fact, a prospective client. He invited me for a chat as he lived close by and I could go on my bike. I'd passed my driving test at the age of 37 not long before, but cars were beyond my budget then.

He didn't tell me before the meeting—and there's no reason why he should—that he was blind. I'm slightly ashamed that it was my first experience up close with a blind person. I remember being amazed by his spatial awareness when he asked me to sit down. I thought "he couldn't know I was standing up, could he?" I immediately had enormous respect for him.

He lived with his mother and brother in a house in rural Brittany and had set up the business in a small room that served as a home office. I was one of his first sub-contractors.

He gave me some work, my first (and only) medical translation, and I attacked it with gusto and my school Harrap's French/English dictionary I'd kept since 1977—this was 1996. The days before Alta Vista, let alone Google.

Looking back now, I have to question my sanity taking on a translation in a subject of which I knew nothing, but I suppose that's one of the things about starting. You don't know what you don't know, and you roll with the punches.

I was just happy to be earning some money from the fruits of my labour for the first time in three and a half years. In those days before generalised electronic file delivery systems, I continued my 30-minute bike ride (and 30 minutes back) to deliver work on floppy disks.

We'd chat, have a cup of coffee, and sometimes even have a spot of lunch. No wonder I didn't get much done in those days. But I was up and running. I was earning money for the first time ages and my self-esteem was on the way up.

How do you summarise more than 25 years of self-employment?

In a nutshell, quickly. It sounds quaint now, but my marketing consisted of writing letters to all the translation agencies in Paris whose addresses I got from old phone books with a CV. It was 1997 and probably the last time I've used a CV.

I was surprised that some wrote back and offered me work and even more surprised when they paid me. Then they called back to ask me to do more. I thought I might be onto something here.

I somehow found my feet and got busy, so by the end of 1997, I was starting to lose my expert skills in Solitaire that I'd honed while waiting for the phone to ring in the previous year.

I had an old second (third? or fourth?) hand IBM PS/2 with a 12-inch screen. It weighed a ton. I used to tap with two fingers unproductively because I'd never learned to touch type. I grew up at a time when girls learned to type if they did secretarial training and boys did woodwork.

I worked with many international conglomerates as a translator: primarily internal documents, contracts from time to time, and technical stuff. I can tell you things about the inside of a tyre you don't want to know. I felt out of my depth sometimes because I knew the terminology I was using but had no real clue about the processes I was involved in.

Most of the documents a translator works on are written by engineers or marketers, or someone similar with no experience in writing. And that is the translator's dilemma. We can cajole and polish meaning from a text, but there's only so much you can do. Every translator has a horror story.

I remember the 9,000-word document on the construction sector I was sent early on without a single punctuation mark. My daughter was six at the time and pointed out spelling and conjugation errors.

Speaking two languages doesn't make you a translator. It's a skill I learned on the job. Good translators are writers in their target languages and mother-tongue speakers. They have to know the nooks and crannies of the languages they are translating towards. They need to know its idiosyncrasies and its strange quirks. They need the deep knowledge that only a lived experience can give.

Native speakers with two mother tongues have grown up bilingual, naturally jumping from one language to another and have never had to take lessons. Speaking two languages is one of the greatest gifts you can give your children.

I also learned at a time when the internet was just getting

started. Search engines were rudimentary, and dial-up came with 40 or 60 hours of access a month, so we had to use our time efficiently.

I spent many an hour in university libraries looking up and compiling terminology in notebooks I kept to hand. I augmented my Harrap's French English dictionary with a couple of Thesauruses and specialist business, legal and a slew of industry-specific works that still sit on my bookshelf, well-thumbed but unused these days.

And so started self-employment. I couldn't go back now even if somebody wanted me because I've got too used to structuring my days exactly how I please. If I want to lie in bed a bit later, I can; if I want to start at 5 am and finish at three or four, I can; if I want to take a day off and work the weekend, I can. That was the new way of working, even before the crisis of 2020 kicked in.

Eventually, most of my work's overly technical subject matter became boring and I got sick of translating other people's bad French. I've morphed in the last ten years or so into a copywriter. I've attended more than 1000 face-to-face networking meetings all over the country, met interesting and not so interesting people and built a business that feeds not only me but my soul.

I'm a lucky bugger really.

Chapter 5

Why People Start Businesses In The First Place

Get a job with good pay and you'll be okay

That's what they say. But is the middle-class dream all it's cracked up to be? We all come into this with our problems and strengths.

The so-called happy middle-class upbringing brings with it all kinds of pressure to achieve. Our parents and teachers told us to get good grades to get a good job—preferably in a bank—find a suitable mate, get married and have children so the entire cycle could start again.

Since the beginning of the twentieth century, those beliefs have fuelled generations as the critical driver of growth. They're portrayed as a prerequisite for a happy life. If you get a job in a bank, train as a doctor, or work for the government, at least you'll get a good pension, something secure. Something that will mean you can live your life in the little spare time you have left over in the evening or at the weekend. And if you can't live your life in your spare time, there's always retirement to look forward to.

A few years ago, I had a 30-something life coach client. He targeted people like him who'd done everything they were told to do at school. By the time they got to their early 30s, they'd got good jobs and grown families just like they's been told. But then they thought, "what's next?" Is it going to be like this for the rest of my life? Another 35 years and then retire? What's the point?

My father was of a generation who spent an entire career not just in the same industry but in the same company. He started on the railways in the late 1940s in the ticket office at the small station in Headstone Lane in Middlesex on the West Coast Main Line out of London. Apart from a break for 18 months of National Service in Singapore, he stayed on the railways until 1985. He was the assistant project manager on the rebuilding of Euston in London in the 1960s and the project manager when Birmingham International was built to serve the newly opened National Exhibition Centre in the mid-70s. He also ran British Rail's first project to lay phone lines along the railway track in the 80s. After he officially retired at 55, he worked as a consultant on railway projects in South Africa and Malaysia to finish an entire career in trains. That world is no more.

Someone I was at school with spent an entire career working at the same hospital and has now retired. My daughter has had at least as many jobs as me, and she's only 32. But I had five jobs before I went freelance at 39. And I'd spent three years of that time unemployed for training to be a teacher. We stay in jobs for much shorter periods than we used to. By the time we get to three or four years, we get itchy feet.

There is no such thing as a secure job these days. Accountants and management consultants ensure companies do all they can to cut the fat. Your job could be at risk at any time. Sometimes the system doesn't play ball because it has its agenda. It seems a job's role is not to give us health and prosperity for the rest of our lives. The generation before me spoke of cradle-to-grave protection, but that turned out to be an illusion. We are in a new world.

30% of businesses set up in the UK between 2011 and 2016 started because the founder had been made redundant. There is a job you can't lose, and it's the one you create yourself.

The stories we tell ourselves and the experiences we have all inform the businesses we create. And by creating those businesses, big or small, we are the outliers and heroes. We are the ones who don't accept the status quo; we are the ones who want to do things on our terms. So, get a secure job? Nah!

Different lives, different expectations

We have different childhoods, we learn differently, and we don't all play the same way. We lead different lives. They are punctuated by the unexpected; the handbrake turns that we look back on and say, "well, that was fun", or just the natural events we all go through. Leaving school, getting a job, all the growing up and living life stuff. We wouldn't have it otherwise. It's what makes us unique.

In my 20s, I never dreamed I'd be working for myself for 25 years. Business ownership wasn't something the careers officer at school told you about. Indeed, I can remember nothing of the one discussion I had with the careers officer in 1976 or 1977.

Of the 30 and 40 or so business owners I spoke to when researching this book, no two had the same story. Some suffered staggering trauma when they were younger, which formed them as adults, and others have seemed to sail through a life where nothing remarkable happens. Or so they think, at least.

Some had a plan all along, but most people work it out as they go. Some are driven by a cause or a belief that the world should be better from an early age, and others are affected by things that happen, and they have wake-up moments that set them on different no paths.

But with only one or two exceptions, they are not made for the 9-to-5 lifestyle. Once they tasted the freedom to choose when and where they worked, they wouldn't return. They've become, in effect, unemployable.

The modern workplace is still organised around the imperatives of the nineteenth-century factory, and attitudes linking being in work to productivity and usefulness to the business remain. If you're there, you must be working. Just look at post-pandemic demands to return to offices for proof of that.

As long ago as 2014, a study by Stanford University showed that staying long hours is no guarantee of productivity. Indeed, productivity declined sharply after 50 hours and fell off a cliff after 55 hours. You are no more productive working 70 hours a week than at 55.

The French saw this many years ago and reduced the working week from 39 to 35 hours with no drop in productivity. A perfect illustration of Parkinson's Law, work expands to fit the time.

Even though organisations are more aware of this than they were, "presenteeism" is still a powerful force, particularly in the US and the UK. As I write this, Elon Musk is demanding staff commit to working longer and longer hours at Twitter. It's probably not surprising that many people want out. So, why do people do it? What's the trigger?

Official statistics say that 15.3% of the UK workforce is self-employed. It's twice that in the US. And the prevailing economic uncertainty is only going to mean that figure will increase.

Sometimes working for ourselves is forced upon us, but mostly the decision is a long time in the making and involves a good amount of fear. Journalist and writer Rebecca Seal left her job with a good cushion to fall back on, but that didn't stop her from agonising for months before taking the leap.

Any leap into the unknown is scary; our fight-or-flight responses inherited from our ancestors have ensured that. But once the decision has been made, and we've decided to strike out, it's exhilarating.

By choosing not to be part of the 9-to-5, to work on our terms, with the people we choose and in conditions we decide, we are the heroes. We are the change-makers. And that, in essence, is what this book is all about.

The five reasons we start businesses

My entirely unscientific survey of the people I have spoken to, asked on social media or in person has revealed five reasons why people start businesses.

Some always had a plan, they always wanted to run a business at some stage or other, and any time they spent working for other people beforehand was just training. They were waiting for the right opportunity and knew what they wanted to do when they grew up. They're not necessarily in the game for fame and fortune but have a vocation. They're in love with what they do. They're craftspeople, writers, or artists and run businesses as much as anyone else.

We don't always have the opportunity of knowing what we want (or wanted) to do when we grow up. Life is a yellow brick road. We sometimes have lions, tin men or scarecrows for companionship, but ultimately, we steer our path with our tools.

I used to joke well into my 50s that I was still working out what I wanted to do when I grew up. That was more deflection than I was prepared to admit at the time, but many people have a clear idea of what they want to do with their lives from a young age.

Accidental entrepreneurs, business owners often made redundant from a previous job who continued their trade because they liked it too much or because it's all they knew. There were also people like me who found themselves with no source of income and thought, "what do I know how to do?"

Accidental entrepreneurs grow to love the independence. Some are happy to stay freelancers, making enough money to maintain their lifestyle, but others want more. They grow businesses, sometimes big ones.

The much-derided "lifestyle business" is not the preserve of stay-at-home mothers. Many set up businesses to work around their home lives. I know of bricklayers who do the hours they need to do in the morning so they can play golf in the afternoon. They have lifestyle businesses just as much as a mother of toddlers selling pamper products.

Lifestyle businesses generally, although not exclusively, exist to provide the owner with a level of income or to maintain a particular lifestyle, and no more than that. There is no desire to grow or conquer the world, but owners want to live their lives on their terms equally. They get derided by some as "not real businesses", but of course, they are. Who can blame anyone for carving out the life they want to live? Many people in corporate booths and grey offices worldwide would bite their hands off for such an existence.

Some people find themselves in untenable work situations.

They don't get along with their boss or colleagues, they're under excessive pressure to produce results, or the atmosphere is just toxic. The obvious solution here is to get another job, but that's often not practical, so the quickest way is to start a business.

Business is also a force for good and solving many of the world's problems. Many people passionately believe in the things they do and what they are building. The real reasons we set up businesses are intrinsically linked to our individual stories. The ones we tell ourselves and the ones we're told. Then events and circumstances conspire to push us into situations where we have to jump of the invisible cliff and launch ourselves into a world we could not perceive before but to which we are well-suited and we soon realise is our natural home.

For some of us, it's a destiny

Deep down, Kira Hug always knew she'd work for herself one day; she just didn't know how. She was the creative one in the family and logically became an Arts student at college. As president of her sorority at Virginia Tech, she says with all the moving parts she had to negotiate, it was just like running a business.

She had her first introduction to advertising when promoting jobs at the university. That was when she fell in love with marketing. She got the bug early on.

As soon as she graduated from Virginia Tech she headed straight to New York City. She got a great introduction to the world of work and marketing with Enterprise Rent-A-Car but as much as she learned, it wasn't what she wanted.

So she moved on to Estée Lauder. The "fancy job" as she

calls it, living the dream of working with architects using her design background? Surely, this was it?

She was getting closer; she wasn't there yet. Although she wanted her business, she felt she was still young and needed just a little more experience before taking the leap. Estée Lauder was too big to get the experience she wanted, so she had to move.

Not one prone to impulsiveness, she makes rational decisions. The end goal was clear, and she had to make a change. There was no drama, no glasses or plates were thrown against the wall, she just needed to move on to new things. So she took on a couple of marketing roles in small nonprofits managing teams and running events, the marketing, websites, the lot. She was constantly testing and probing.

She wasn't short of ideas and spent her time trying to imagine what her business would look like. Eventually, she found a startup where she was doing marketing and writing copy. More and more people began hiring her to write. Then a friend she'd been working for pointed out to her she was, in fact, a copywriter. Bingo, she'd found her business. Perhaps it had been there all along, hiding in plain sight. There was a transition period from her employed status to freelance—cautious Kira again—but she needed little persuasion to leap.

She proceeded gradually and carefully, doing many hours trying to juggle both jobs, but Kira is thorough and wanted to do things right. She joined Joanna Wiebe's Copy Hackers mastermind in 2015, where she met Rob Marsh and several other now well-established copywriters.

On the surface, everything separates Kira and Rob; age, temperament and location—they live on opposite sides of the US, her in Portland, Maine where she moved from Washington DC in 2020 and him in Salt Lake City. But they hit it off. The best business partnerships are between people who are polar opposites and Kira says she wants a partner who can do the things she can't.

They started by setting up a podcast called the Copywriter Club, where copywriters discuss their trade and craft. They then launched a Facebook group to help copywriters connect. Paid programs were a natural development for the group. The business is going from straight to strength with masterminds, courses and in-person events whenever they can.

Kira knew she'd end up with a business but didn't know what it would be. She wasn't "called" to writing as a profession, but discovered it along the way. She found her business in the end and it makes her happy in her work being able to make a difference. Who would argue with her?

Like Neely Khan, like Amy Harrison, they knew there was something to them that would lead.

Conversely, Rebecca Seal loved writing from a young age but never envisaged it as a career. She comes from a family of social workers and was top of the class all through school. Her family background taught her that work should involve "something exceptional in public service." This led her to the London School of Economics and a degree in International Development.

It was only later when international development didn't particularly have a job for her, that she turned to hospitality and then journalism that she found her love. She wrote a book about working solo and discusses what it is to do meaningful work. It turns out that writing is a meaningful job too, and she can make a difference with it. Again, two wildly different paths but the same outcome.

There's a debate about whether entrepreneurs are born or made. Kira, Neely, Amy or even Rebecca don't necessarily fit the model, but they share some traits. They are independent and rarely troubled by self-doubt about why they do what they do, at least. They don't want to be dependent on anyone for their income. They want to make life the centre of what they do and let work fit around it rather than the other way around. It's a question of priority.

You can't prepare for everything

Sometimes, when we think work is the centre of things, life comes in and throws a spanner in the works. Previously, people had to give up a promising career, a well-paid job in a toxic work environment or how to reconcile the demands of a family and those of work. But now we have options.

When a young Michelle Dalley was climbing up the corporate ladder, she had no idea she would end up running a food marketing business from her home on an old farm in South Wales. She never had a plan about what she wanted to do when she grew up. But she knew school did not inspire her and couldn't wait to leave and get a job. She had no truck with the standard careers advice you got in the late 80s—doctor, nurse, secretary. Sixteen or seventeen is no age to realise the world needs all kinds of skills and professions beyond the obvious marquee ones that everyone imagines. So she looked elsewhere.

She's a grafter and something of a force of nature who goes through life with a permanent smile. She was young and wanted to be doing things; she didn't want to hang around waiting for something to happen.

She fell into the food industry by chance after walking into a job centre and taking the first job on offer. And the rest, as they say, is history. Despite being a vegetarian, she worked for a catering company that sold meat to restaurants. She always loved work and says she can't think of a time when she truly hated her job.

Unlike many other business owners I've spoken to, she's never felt like a square peg in a round hole. She fitted perfectly into the structure and the rules because she knew how to play them. If there was a role or a job she wanted, she positioned herself so she could do it. And she was good, so she got what she wanted.

She took the next step often before she was ready because she had the confidence to do so. The only plan she had was that next step. When she was 16, she noticed sales reps had company cars; she had one by 21. There wasn't a plan; she just took opportunities when they presented themselves. She remembers thinking she didn't want to struggle. And despite her success, she thinks of herself as 'ordinary'. She just wanted to enjoy her job. And if there were things she didn't enjoy, she had the strength of character to change them. She made herself indispensable—not in a threatening manner; it was just a positioning strategy. She's grateful that throughout her corporate career, she got the support to do the things she wanted. She had bosses who believed in her and knew she would deliver.

Having a family hadn't been in the plan either. Until it was. But in true Michelle fashion, she planned to have her son go on maternity leave and then return to her corporate job. But life isn't that clear-cut. There are always forks in the road and things to knock us off track. She'd never stopped for more than ten days for a holiday or prolonged sickness.

But suddenly, she was at home with a different life. It too, was a life she lived to the full. She started worrying about what she would miss if she went back to work and about the constant push and pull of family life. She realised she didn't want to be a part-time mother missing out on sports days, parents' evenings, or any other crucial part of her son's life. But she didn't want to give up work either. She couldn't have combined being a senior account manager in one of the biggest food companies in hospitality and the school play on a Tuesday afternoon. So she went for the hybrid option.

Her husband, Haddon, already ran a successful design business, so she joined him. Initially, Michelle learned about design and websites, and they found a balance in their skills. Michelle's expertise is in food and customers, and Haddon's is in websites and design. And it works.

There's no tradition of running a business in her family, but her 15 years in corporate have served her well. She has an inexhaustible capacity for work, and she's been able to exploit her network to work with terrific brands and companies, making her mark in the world and thoroughly enjoying it.

It hasn't always been perfect. She's worked with the wrong clients for too little money, and she's also worked with the wrong clients for large amounts of money. She has to pay the mortgage. Over the last 12 years, she's developed her own identity in the business specialising in food marketing and now is an outsourced director for several sizeable brands.

She's not troubled by self-doubt and says she doesn't do guilt either. When there's something to be done for work, she goes ahead and does it, and the family carries on just fine.

She's not one for overthinking too much, so when the pandemic hit, she had two days of panic and, as she says, "got bored with that" and cracked on. "I have very little patience with myself for things like that", which is not to denigrate anyone with panic issues or anything related. She's simply not like that.

Her son has grown up balanced and happy. He's grown up

with her mental resilience, which will serve him well in the future. He's also pretty good at sports with excellent hand-eye coordination, so Michelle's spent a lot of time playing taxi and being a spectator around the football, rugby and cricket pitches of South Wales over the years. I walked into her in Bristol a few months ago on a weekday afternoon with her young, now 13-year-old in tow. That's the freedom she's carved out for herself.

When independent thought and towing the company line come into conflict

She might not want me to say it, but Margo Aaron is one hell of a human being. She's the product of her story, and more than almost anyone I know, she uses her experience to move forward and improve. "I love life", she told me on a Zoom call a few months ago.

Born and raised in a Jewish family in Texas, she was encouraged from a young age to be open to other people and other worlds and to see how they lived and what they did. Her grandfather was a Holocaust survivor and she takes her name from his sister Margot who was gassed as a teenager in Auschwitz, along with his parents and 60-odd other family members. As she grew up, she was imbued with the idea that her life should matter and that she could be someone—the American Dream. That works, she says, "until you realise the other side of the coin is thinking you're not good enough." "Both following the dream and having doubts are human, and both are fine. But there's a culture that tells us you are not enough. And I think that got mixed up with my genuine desire to do more."

She travelled a lot when she was young and saw parts of the world that other kids never got to see. She found when she got back, she and her peers weren't interested in the same things. That contributed to her sense of being another, of being different. But like any other teenager and young adult, she wanted to fit in and be part of the crowd. She wanted friends and to be popular. "I was tired of being the weird one," she said.

"Where (being different) became most apparent was when I took my first job out of college because all the other jobs I'd worked before didn't seem real. My (previous) full-time identity was student. I didn't have that gravity with other jobs. Other people talk about where they needed to make money to pay the bills, and even if I did (too), I still didn't identify that way; I always identified as a student. My job was getting good grades, learning and growing; the money was tangential. But I also had the privilege of having parents that helped. So that was a big part of it financially".

Something went awry in the transition from college into the real world of work. Margo started thinking something was wrong because she wanted to do things differently. The nine-to-five made little sense to her at all. She couldn't reconcile the need to carve out time for herself, so she could be physically healthy, eat right and move, and simultaneously sacrifice everything in the name of ambition and high achievement.

Life was full of contradictions. She had to think independently and obey a boss to get ahead. She had to "be healthy" but work 15 hours a day "and eat the candy in the break room and make sure you go to happy hour; otherwise, people are gonna think you're weird. You need to simulate, but also be independent-minded socially" She missed opportunities by opting out.

If she questioned the system, the people around her made her feel like the entitled millennial stereotype and afraid of hard work. She's not; far from it.

She wondered if she saw things other people didn't want to see. She felt compelled to play the game for a boss and colleagues she didn't particularly care for in a system that didn't suit her just to climb the greasy pole. But to what end? A company car, an annual pay rise and a picket fence in a suburb? That American Dream? "I was deeply unhappy, very stressed out, and I was contorting myself to fit into a world that wasn't conducive to independent thought. And I was thinking that I wasn't being independent; I thought that I was being difficult."

That happens in corporate jobs to people who want to stand out. She worked in a depression clinic, interviewing depressed people about their condition, and she worked in marketing strategy before she fell into copywriting almost accidentally. Following a bouncing ball, as she puts it.

It wasn't until she started to look elsewhere that she realised things didn't need to be like that. She joined Ramit Sethi's Brain Trust and she met the people who were able to combine going out drinking with friends and personal growth. It was an also there she learned about Seth Godin and the altMBA. She realised other people thought like her. Almost for the first time, she felt part of the crowd. She'd found her "people."

"What," she thought, "there are other people out there who think like me?" And gradually, the idea of having a business on her terms started to take hold. If there's anyone who's proudly unemployable, it's Margo.

Although she's under no illusion that she can only make a small contribution to the world, she's sure as hell going to make it count for as much as she can. She wants to make her mark and believes things can improve. It's easy for us to look back now and see the patterns, but things weren't so apparent then. In the workplace, she was making herself smaller to fit in. She thought she could change the system from within, as a researcher, as a professor or within a corporate structure. She tried hard to fit in but wouldn't compromise her values.

She was too curious for her own good sometimes. "I remember there was optional continuing education provided when I was in corporate. You could learn about finance, for example. I wanted to know, and I was a strategist at the time. And I remember my co-strategists asking me why I cared and how the company runs the CPG arm. "It's not relevant to your trajectory", they'd say.

"I couldn't understand that perspective. I wanted to know how the company was run. I wanted to know how the whole thing plays together. They didn't understand."

Company people were there to stay in their lanes and silos and chase that dream of so-called "prosperity." They were never to diverge until it was time to retire and somehow enjoy life. "I'm highly sensitive, but my nervous system is just different. My brain will get just so consumed."

When she finally did strike out on her own, she went through the same struggles. At Seth Godin's suggestion, she wrote a copywriting course "in the traditional way" in lecture format with rave reviews from all her students. They gave her excellent testimonials. She was incredibly proud of what she had put out. She thought how she explained everything was revolutionising the teaching of copywriting. In the end, she asked her students to send her some copy. "And it was garbage. They were better at talking about copy; they felt more confident in understanding it intellectually, but no one had improved how they wrote copy."

"And I went back to Seth and told him it didn't work" She says that Seth said, like an old sage, "Come to me, child", with a benign smile on his face (note: he probably didn't say that, it was just Margo's characterisation of the great man's style).

So she returned to the drawing board and started building a different program where students couldn't get away with not doing the work and couldn't phone it on subjects they thought they knew. It would be a program with no right or wrong answers; students would have to work out the answers independently. The altMBA works the same way; it uses prompts that get students thinking with no lessons and no tests. And it works well even if it is disconcerting to some people stuck in the traditional ways. Working that way was made for Margo.

She's still working things out. She draws on many different cultures. She says that technically she's American, but that's only on her father's side. But her mother's side is Israeli and a grand European tradition before that. She's a citizen of the world and is very conscious of her place in it. She worries about her role as a mother and a business owner and how those two identities intertwine. I should introduce her to my friend Michelle Dalley to reassure her that things can work out well.

Life must have a purpose. She doesn't want to find herself "living in this world of riches, but I am dead inside." When she left Texas for New Jersey in her late teens, she felt she was moving towards something she needed to find. Now she's moved to Kansas City as a 30-something mother; she feels she can have an influence and is in the driving seat. That's a pretty good place to be.

The point of a business is to do some good

Gemma Roe left school with no qualifications. She says she was the creative non-academic one in the family who should have gone to a Steiner School, where she would have fared better than in a traditional one. All she wanted to do was paint, draw, sing and dance. It used to be a bit of a running joke in her family, "you know, Gemma's the arty one."

So she left without any qualifications and got a job. She worked in offices and took the traditional "career path" that her upbringing had told her to follow. Working and using her talents to pick up the skills she needed, by her mid-20s, she'd managed to carve out a promising career in finance with all the trimmings and trappings. For someone who left school with nothing, she'd not done so badly.

But when she got to the stage where she'd achieved what she wanted, Gemma hit a wall and wondered what the next challenge would be. Had she embarked on a 30-year path to retirement? Was that to be her life? She wanted more than that.

So she returned to her creative roots and studied to be an interior designer. She got the bug with the eco-building industry. Suddenly, it all made sense. She's not only found a role in life but a purpose too.

After her three-year course, she became co-director of a company building eco-friendly homes. She was a 5% minority shareholder, so she didn't consider herself a *bona fide* business owner at that point, but the business appeared on Dragon's Den (Shark Tank on the other side of the Atlantic) and got an offer of investment. They decided to walk away from the deal but although the appearance was scary, getting investment was a significant confidence builder and made her realise there was something in her ideas.

At the same time, she discovered I was pregnant. She'd felt the company she worked for wasn't the perfect fit for her for a while, so it seemed like the ideal opportunity to leave. That's how she found herself at her kitchen table with an idea and, luckily enough, another investor who believed in her. It was one of those "gulp" sink or swim moment. She could have taken the easy route, as many of her friends told her, and taken the benefit payments. No, she saw it as an opportunity to design something that fit her aspirations.

Since reading Bruce Hudson's *Go it Alone* and realising employment is a trap, she'd always wanted to run a business. She didn't know what it would be, but it would be on her terms. The more she researched the idea of living in round houses and discovered the positive psychological impact, the more it became a cause. It had to be her business too.

At the time, she couldn't have imagined another option. It was so clear that she would carry on and make a success of it. Otherwise, she and her child would live in poverty forever. The idea of not being able to support her child was a great motivator, and she helped her Rotunda Roundhouses business to survive. A single mother at her kitchen table, she had nothing to lose; she would leverage all her knowledge.

She was confident from a young age; she'd made it as a young woman in a world of finance dominated by middle-aged white men. Circumstances landed her in a position where she was unemployed at the kitchen table with a new baby and nothing else. She had nothing to lose. As a single mum with a child, the options were to sit on the benefits system indefinitely, get a job and find childcare five days a week or design her own business to fit her lifestyle.

She stayed on benefits for a couple of years before she could draw a salary, and now, ten years later, the business is sustainable and helps 20 people or so live, pay their mortgages and achieve their dreams.

In many ways, Gemma's story is typical of entrepreneurs, the single mother on benefits who "started on the kitchen table" and grew a sustainable and profitable business over ten years.

She lives her passion for eco-building, especially living in round buildings.

She believes business can and should be a force for good. She's built hers to the point where it can stand independently and is now devoting some of her energy to different causes.

Gemma passionately believes in building homes differently. She says our current system is broken, with major house builders only interested in the balance sheet. Any concern for sustainability, energy saving or whether homes are pleasant to live in is surface-level only. "They're not interested in how the building feels and acts to residents. They're not thinking about the long-term impacts on the environment. They're just thinking about putting a structure up and making as much money as possible. I think that is deplorable (...) they should be building for people and the planet. And then profits come after that. Yeah. So that's the mission that I'm on now. We can go home and develop for first-time buyers"

She also believes that if you can't get the job that suits you best, it should be possible to make it for yourself. So many people get herded into career paths by parents or teachers when they are young and find it difficult to break out of them because they're not aware of the possibilities at that age.

So she wrote a book to help as many people as possible realise they can escape the 9-to-5 and achieve the independence they've always craved. She's used her experience of not being able to get the job she wanted and then making one. She now mentors young business owners, helping them grow businesses to do good in the world.

It took a catastrophic event to slingshot her into action. People with the least to lose take the greatest risks, and she's not sure she would do it the same way now because she has more to lose. But that's not a reason not to take the leap. She had a recurring dream about walking her through a tree house rotunda when her daughter was a small baby. Then, when her daughter reached the age of 7, she was commissioned by her very own primary school to build an outdoor classroom. They called it the tree house.

Einstein said imagination is more important than knowledge because knowledge limits you to what you know, and imagination leaves you with things to find out. Gemma had a vision and a positive feeling. She just knew.

Harriet Randall has a different type of cause but perhaps with the same outcome

There's a lot of snobbery about a "real business" just as much as there is about "real jobs" Much of it is promoted by the likes of Dragon's Den, Shark Tank and The Apprentice. A business must make something, provide goods or services. It can't be something people do for a hobby. Harriet has turned what people told her was her hobby, the thing that has guided her all her life, into a real business that pays the bills. She helps people dance. On the surface at least, because the effects go much further than that. More on that later.

No two lives are the same, and no two businesses are the same. Whatever your background, or circumstances, if your business is up and running, it's legit.

I don't think Harriet will mind me saying she was a regular young girl. She had a routine, relatively comfortable upbringing. She was on track for great things. Like many young girls her age, she wanted to be a dancer. Often against her parents' wishes. It was a passion. She can't remember what triggered it, but it seems like it's been with her forever.

It was more than just a schoolgirl obsession with ballerinas.

She was mad about dance. It never left her. Indeed, it still hasn't. It even survived a teacher telling her she didn't have the right body to be a dancer.

But she grew up a sensible girl from a sensible family. And that family didn't share her passion. They didn't understand that it was what she just had to do. They thought she'd grow out of it and get a "real" job with a salary, pension and prospects. They wanted her to have a career path and a life plan. Something safe. They told her dancing wasn't a job with prospects. Some prima ballerinas at the Royal Ballet may disagree.

So she did the sensible thing, went to Oxford, no less, and got a degree in Spanish and Italian. Being surrounded by all those aspiring lawyers and management consultants made her even more determined not to become one. The thought of spending a lifetime cooped up in an office was not in her plans. Things weren't going well for the "sensible job" option.

At university, she got involved in small dance events and choreographed several presentations. It was in her mind to do a Masters' degree in dance, but then her brother said that dance was just a hobby and she should get a job. The family again. So she did.

Some things won't go away once they get into your head. Harriet still wanted to work in dance. She got a glamorous-sounding job working in industrial intelligence. Except she hated it and left after less than a year.

She got some experience in event management at a local exhibition centre and then made it to the Birmingham Royal Ballet to coordinate events. Surely, this was it?

Well, not exactly. She stayed at the Royal Ballet for 18 months but quit when the depression and anxiety just got too much. Our mutual friend Vicky Quinn Fraser, among others, told her that life was too short to stay in a job that made her ill. And they were right; there are a few things worse than going to a job you hate every day.

She met Vicky at burlesque classes. Vicky then not only taught her pole dancing, but she encouraged her to set up as a VA when her job was getting too much. Harriet went to Spain as a language consultant, creating resources for people to use in schools, and the idea of running her own business started to take hold. She'd posted some videos of her burlesque routines online, and a friend asked her if she'd consider teaching them.

She says it was a couple of years before she took the idea seriously and started posting regular content and developing her online school. Her school is a major part of her life; she's achieved her dream. But she still suffers from imposter syndrome. She still wonders whether it's her place to be teaching dance because, after all, it's just dance. It's frivolous. It's a hobby.

She says, "I think the difficulty is that what I do for everybody—apart from the teachers—is a hobby; it's fun for them. People don't take it seriously. But also me, I think but also for you, I'm just doing this silly thing. I'm teaching people routines."

What may be your or my hobby is someone else's vocation or the thing that saves them from depression. Who's to say what's a "real job" or what isn't?

She underplays how she helps people. She gives them an outlet; she's part of their quality of life and nurturing their passion. These are the kind of things that make us human.

A year after I first wrote this, Harriet is about to leave her VA life behind and plunge head-first into burlesque. She says she has to do it because that is her mission in life. She'll be fine.

In the end, fundamentally unemployable

Although she took a while to realise it, like the rest of us, Laura Hall is fundamentally unemployable. She was a magazine editor in her mid-20s when she decided she could do better than the writers she was editing, many of whom wrote for national papers. She admits to being quite competitive and used the image of someone not being quite as good as she thought they ought to be as fuel.

Laura's always been interested in how we interact. When she was young, she loved writing and reading and worked for her local newspaper at 15. She knew she would be a journalist or a writer, but she was interested in more than that. She says she can write a good sentence with the right words in the right order, but that's not enough. Any idiot can do that. Content needs to have a message and a purpose; it needs to make a point. It's her primary weapon in studying people and how they behave.

She studied English at Oxford and moved to London to learn about journalism. She landed a succession of jobs in branding and marketing, ping-ponging between working freelance and working for a salary.

The important part of her work is telling a great story that makes a difference to someone and touches them. Much of it has been in the travel industry but doesn't mean writing about what people did on their holidays. While it may be true for some writers, even a cursory look at some great travel writing shows it's about much more. She feels her job is encouraging people to visit parts of the world that will change their view of life.

"When I'm writing about and working with travel, I'm thinking about how to help support a local community. How do we make sure that tourists' experiences are authentic? So they can go back to their home country and think what they did was amazing? Can they use it as an enriching opportunity?"

She lives in Denmark now and, until recently, worked as the head of English content at the Danish Tourist Board. But ultimately, as great as the job was talking about Denmark and telling stories about the place and its people, she realised that the office environment was not for her. She didn't want to deal with the petty rivalries and the backbiting. Life is too short for that.

She now runs a small English-speaking writing agency in Copenhagen, working with travel and lifestyle brands alongside brands looking to be change makers.

Living in a different culture is one of the most enriching things you can do. But especially when you are learning the language, it has its problems. "The best experiences we've had in getting to know the cultures is to do it with a three-year-old and a seven-year-old. They went to a Danish school, and I met all the other parents. At the first birthday party my three-year-old went to, everybody was obviously Danish, and nobody spoke English. Everyone was singing crazy birthday songs, and I was like a rabbit in the headlights." She had to apologise to people for not speaking Danish, but she'd love to talk to them because she had no clue what was happening. "And they took me under their wings. I think it just got adopted by that parent group." They decided they needed to show Laura what was happening, and I felt like I was part of a family. She's gained a few terrific friends; they spotted her as a fish out of water and got her through. "I think that enormous kindness integrates into this culture."

Her children are bilingual, but she can't help with homework. That's just one of the things parents who move around have to face; their kids will pick up the language quicker than they do. But integration into a foreign language and culture has been one of the most enriching experiences of her life. She thinks it's important, where possible, to live the best life you can and, if you have the talents to do so, make a difference with them.

Like me, she tries to juggle two languages and two cultures. The family speaks English at home and watches the BBC, but it's a part-time life in two languages. When she speaks Danish, people think she's Swedish. I'm not sure she realises how much of a compliment that is. She lives in a world where everyone speaks good English and another language, too—they understand the idioms and the jokes. It makes her feel inadequate.

She wants the business to be something she feels comfortable doing, sustainable projects and work with people who are not dicks. She seems to be getting there.

And it doesn't stop her from living life to the full. Her Instagram feed is full of pictures of her freshwater swimming and travelling to stunning places across Scandinavia and Greenland. She's currently writing a book about that. Watch this space.

Chapter 6

The Stuff That Gets In The Way Of The Story

It's probably time to rehabilitate failure.

We like to be successful because we perceive that others like us more like that. Our ego takes credit for the effort we put in, our skills, or our experience. Consequently, research shows we're more likely to claim internal factors are behind our successes. If things go right, it's all on us.

Failure, though, is never our fault. We'll blame external factors like bad luck, incompetence in others or sometimes just the bad weather.

It's natural human emotion and reaction to situations. At some point, we've all thought we were going to fail. Fail exams, fail in relationships, fail in business and hell, fail in life.

Fear of failure is a reaction that dates back to the days of the sabre-toothed tiger. Our genetics mean that being labelled a failure puts us in perceived mortal danger if we mess things up. The fear of being rejected by the group is the same because the group is our support network; without it, we are nothing.

Our parents are there to "protect" us from failure and arguably are far more aware of this than we think. Robert Plant tells the story of his parents telling him a job was still open at an accountancy firm in Wolverhampton well after Led Zeppelin's first album had become a massive hit in 1969.

In my early years in France, my father convinced me to go back to London to interview for the British Rail Graduate Training Scheme because he believed that, as I was 23, I should be on the path to a career. I failed the interview spectacularly, and I promise I didn't do it deliberately.

We all know we learn from failure, but few of us do. We condemn ourselves to make the same mistakes time and time again. It's a short leap from failure to finding fault. If there's been a mistake, then someone has to be to blame. There's not a child or a lowly (because it's always the lowly ones) employee who hasn't felt that at some stage. It's why we fetishise failure so much, and our culture hasn't given us enough space to examine why a particular fault or mistake happened.

In her famous study on mindset, Carol Dwek concluded that the world is divided into two. Some people have a fixed mindset, and others have a growth one. The former comprises people who view setbacks and failure as part of life. They expect them because they have reached their ceiling and can't go any further. Their mindset is set in stone. This is not limited to people we would consider "unsuccessful." Lee Iacocca is credited with turning around Chrysler Motors when it was on the brink of collapse. But once the company was back in the black, he changed. He considered his job was done, and he started putting more energy into his image as "the man who saved Chrysler" rather than moving from straight to strength. Clearly a fixed mindset.

A growth mindset draws on the lessons of failure. Rather

than seeing failure as a disaster, people with a growth mindset see it as an opportunity. Failure is inevitable on the path to success. It took me a long time to realise that, and my failures were a source of great shame for a long time.

In a 2014 TED talk, "The power of believing you can improve", Carol Dwek looks at school grades and the finality of Passes and Fails. When a child starts to learn to walk and falls for the first time, it doesn't think it's not meant to walk; it doesn't think walking is for other kids and grown-ups. No, like all the others, it gets up repeatedly until it's learned. So, rather than saying "fail", how about saying "not yet?" It gives us hope.

What we put in the way of success has everything to do with personal narrative. For years, I was on my dynamic of failure, a self-fulfilling prophecy that meant I needed one hell of a kick up the backside to snap out of it. Failure doesn't have to breed failure.

Gerald Ratner is the poster boy for spectacular cock-ups. But perhaps less known is the way he bounced back. He inherited his family's High Street jewellery business from his father in 1984. By the end of the decade, he'd turned it into a multi-million dollar empire and could seemingly do no wrong. Ratners was where working-class boys went hesitantly to buy their girlfriends not just engagement rings but also trinkets and baubles because they wanted to be nice. It was at the low end of the market, but was hugely successful.

Then, in a speech to the Institute of Directors in 1991, he blew it all up in a few seconds. "People say: 'How can you sell this for such a low price?' I say: 'Because it's total crap'"

"(We) sold a pair of earrings for under a pound, which is cheaper than a shrimp sandwich from Marks and Spencer, but probably wouldn't last as long." It's become so iconic in the UK that comparable business belly-flops are called "doing a Ratner."

The company's share value dropped by £500 million (at 1991 prices) in days, and it never recovered. Within a year, he was out of the picture. The company had to change its name to re-invent itself and go on to bigger and better things. The new company, Signet, is now the world's largest retailer of diamond jewellery.

Soon after the speech, he claimed his words were taken out of context but later owned up. The game was up. He says he spent seven years in bed, in the wilderness, shorn of his playboy lifestyle and struggled with depression. It was only when his wife, Moira, threatened to kick him out that things started to change. He started a health club in Henley-in-Thames—a place only the well-heeled can afford to live—and sold it five years later for £3.9m. He's also run online jewellery businesses but has now built a new career looking at how to recover from adversity. I remember seeing him speak in Bristol a few years ago and was self-deprecating about the whole affair. He's happier now. He's been able to get over his moment of madness and his long period in the wilderness. He regrets what he said but has drawn a line under it.

Most of the time, there is little to be gained from blame because guilt is such a toxic emotion. We all mess up and fail from time to time, and unless no one is hurt, it's best to move on and learn.

The world is not binary, and success and failure are not absolutes. I asked people in several business groups on Facebook what their attitude to failure was. Each of them said it was a learning process or a lesson that served them well for the future. But no one could give any examples. They trotted out the kind of responses that you see in motivational quotes or hear in business seminars.

We are embarrassed by failure and sometimes even ashamed. We let our egos take over when they have no place in making our decisions. The first question to ask, perhaps, is, what does failure mean? We are very good at visualising success, but failure is still a taboo subject. And yet, you can't have one without the other.

When I started writing at the end of 2020 at the behest of Margo Aaron, I wrote several things that had hitherto remained in the lock and key at the back of my mind. These were the things I was ashamed of, including the reasons why I left American Express in 1993 to start a long, dark period of unemployment. I told everyone around me that I'd been made redundant. I hadn't. I was going through a rough time, losing the plot. I was ashamed. No one got hurt, but I seriously took my eye off the ball and ended up in a disciplinary procedure at work, resulting in me leaving by the back door.

That was almost 30 years ago, and I've never told anyone. I realise now that I cocked up, no more, no less. It wasn't a disaster, and I wouldn't be where I am today if it had not happened. Twenty-five years ago, I'd been discussing all my ventures that somehow never made it to fruition with a therapist. My dodgy career choices, lack of direction, and recent failure to qualify as a teacher. He told me I was in a dynamic of failure. Perhaps I didn't hear or understand the bit about how to combat it; I just listened to the word failure. I gave myself a label, just like I did when I was a child, thinking I'd almost killed my parents, and labelled myself as "broken."

I also missed the bit about compassion, being generous with myself and letting my ego go. Our egos are obtuse little buggers and, while useful most of the time, would do well every so often to sit in the corner and shut up. So yes, failure is part of the learning process. But it's only so if we can be generous and compassionate with ourselves to allow it to be.

My life has been a constant battle with a narrative of failure, but I now realise that it is a construct that depends on the criteria and metrics I set. I can move the goalposts. This entire narrative is based on my realisation two years ago that I have a story worth telling. I've learnt things and continue to learn them. I'm touch-typing this book. It's a skill that has eluded me for as long as I've worked for myself. I'm learning Spanish and can now hold a simple conversation but am no longer bothered by the mistakes I make. The process won't be the same for other people, but the principle is the same. Stories with nothing but success are little more than anecdotes. Gerald Ratner's success is only important in light of his spectacular failure. We love the story of the plucky guy who accumulates fiasco after fiasco but wins in the end. Because maybe we do learn from our failures, and it is time to say "not yet."

Paralysis, perfectionism and overthinking, with a special mention for the French assistant

The French assistant Marie-Laure sat in front of me on a stool, pulling on an imaginary string as though she were trying to extract words from me. I was struggling to produce the perfect phrase and didn't want to feel stupid in front of someone much better at French than me.

I was placing the bar far too high because she was French and using her mother tongue. I would never be that good. Not at 17, anyway. She was there to help me improve, but I didn't seem to understand that. So there we were, at an impasse, a standoff, even. I was part of a "big" group of two in a French class in school. I can't remember whether my classmate Barbara had similar problems, but for me, it was torture. I knew what I wanted to say but couldn't find the words. They were somewhere, but I was buggered if I could find them. I even sent out a search party.

She wanted to hear what I had to say, but I wanted the words to appear fully formed. The enormous smile on her face probably did a good job of hiding her frustration. I struggled to find the words that invariably would never come. Stuck on the tip of my tongue ... some of them are probably still there. Eventually, with practice, I got better, and my tongue loosened. Confidence comes with practice. I was better than I thought, but the monkey brain that tried to protect me from ridicule had other ideas for a while.

There were other French assistants at University, the slightly snooty *bon chic bon genre* Parisienne Cécile and the loveable but slightly batty Annie from Normandy. I spoke French with both of them long after I forgot the imperfections of earlier. But later, when I was working in Paris, I'd cringe every time I made a mistake. I wouldn't ask what words meant but try to work them out from the context. I absolutely had to blend into the background. I went native eventually. The result was often being able to pass for French. The downside was that I may have lost myself a little in the process.

It may not be easy to accept, but we can't be perfect every time. There is little point in beating ourselves up because we fall short of nye-on impossible goals. The modern world makes it worse. Thirty years ago, you only saw successful people on TV, in the newspapers or glossy magazines. Now, they're almost impossible to avoid in the online world. Thomas Curran and Andrew Hill's study, *Perfectionism Is Increasing Over Time: A Meta Study of Birth Cohort*

Differences From 1989 to 2016, found significant increases among more recent undergraduates in the US, the UK, and Canada compared to previous generations. The world in which they are growing up is making them increasingly perfectionists.

And that doesn't mean they are getting more accomplished. On the contrary, they are increasingly frustrated that they are not. Perfectionists believe anything short of perfect is unacceptable and not worth doing. They tend to be very sensitive to even the slightest criticism. They overthink everything. I still have perfectionist traits, I still compare my writing of this book to other people's books, and I am, in fact, a world champion over-thinker. You can ask any coach I've ever had and many of my friends.

It's probably a sign of extremely low self-esteem and arrogance to think things have to be right the first time. No one is ever perfect the first time. Just look at any super successful YouTuber, especially the ones whose videos are accomplished and professional looking. They all had to start somewhere, and those who haven't removed their early ones, take a look and see how terrible they were. It's something to give up all hope. After all, what right do we have to be perfect?

When the imposter gremlins come calling

I'll start by saying that I am describing my lived experience only here. It is not a general comment on imposter syndrome; I am not a mental health professional.

Joanna Wiebe at Copy Hackers told me she's never suffered from imposter syndrome. She had no idea what copywriting was when she came to it, so "I didn't put it on a pedestal", I just figured it out. The Lean Start-Up approach to building a business meant that failing was part of the process, so she didn't need to compare herself to other successful people.

But for the rest of us, the struggle is real. In a nutshell, we define imposter syndrome as doubting our abilities and feeling like a fraud. It's that feeling that everyone around you is more successful, skilled, and happier than you are. It can happen to anyone, irrespective of our level of success, but business owners are particularly prone to it.

It was first identified in an article published in 1978 called "*The Impostor Phenomenon in High-Achieving Women: Dynamics and Therapeutic Intervention*" by Pauline R. Clance and Suzanne A. Imes. They described the "impostor phenomenon" as "an internal experience of intellectual phoniness" and initially focused their research on women in higher education and professional industries.

Subsequent research has found that men are just as likely to suffer from it as women. With men, it manifests as the feeling of not being successful or simply not being good enough—probably a throwback to our cave-dwelling years. I spent many years comparing myself to people at the top of their game and not feeling I was "enough." I thought I was definitely "broken" and "bad."

When I was a student with my fantasies of being a history professor, I'd look at the writers of great tomes and authoritative works and think how I'd love to be like them while believing deep down that I'd never become that good.

Then more recently, I'd look at the rock stars of the marketing world and think I could never have their experience and knowledge and somehow, I was not a good person because of that.

How many years did I worry about what other people thought of me and that those thoughts were mostly negative?

How many years did I think everyone else had it all sorted out, and they were ahead of me? I thought terrible things about myself. I knew, deep down, it wasn't good enough. I tried everything, courses, therapy, and every quick fix available. Nothing worked.

I knew that if I put my head above the parapet, I'd get shot down or (worse) ignored. And sure enough, every time I got the nerve to stand out just a little, I got ignored, so I stopped doing it. After all, what's the point? It was a self-fulfilling prophecy.

I stayed in my lane and did conventional things. I carried on doing things I hated, despised myself for doing, or just bored me because they were easy. I didn't know where I was going; I was lost. That's what years of conditioning with imposter syndrome and shame can do for you.

On one occasion, I was in a room with a group of people I knew from face-to-face networking groups. It included people from right across the country, people I considered the "in" crowd and I wasn't one of them. I was on the outside looking in. I mentioned this to Jo Howarth about a year ago, and she remembers it too. She has the same memory as me, except she thinks she was outside looking in, and I was part of the cool gang. She was definitely in the cool gang, but I don't want to argue with her.

Things started turning for me when I realised I wasn't alone. Human beings are comparison ninjas. It's likely the result of our competitive nature, meaning we have to have a benchmark to measure against. Almost everyone feels imposter syndrome at some stage—unless you're Joanna Wiebe.

Although it never goes away entirely, I learned to manage my imposter syndrome when I realised it could be my friend if only I'd let it. It would be scary for a while, but ultimately it was a sign of growth. When I joined Joanna Wiebe's group of successful copywriters, I thought I was entirely out of my depth and in the wrong room. After a while, I realised that these people were trying to run better businesses, just like me. They were no different to me, and I could contribute. Just by recognising its presence, it became less important.

I don't think one particular thing showed me the way out of imposter syndrome and a general lack of confidence and lack of self-belief. It was instead a succession of factors that had the cumulative effect of bringing me belief and confidence.

I discovered I was speaking negatively about myself. It's not something we notice and realise until someone else points it out. It can manifest itself when we say things like "I'm not very good at ..", "I'm an idiot", or all the "shoulds", "woulds", and "coulds" we say all the time.

Just noticing your habit will be most of the work you need to do to correct it. There's no point in berating yourself for speaking negatively; that would defeat the object. A little meditation allowed me to be a little kinder to myself. Simply noticing will mean your ego will have nowhere to go.

In 2018 I read Ryan Holliday's *The Daily Stoic*. It's a series of 365 daily musings on Stoic philosophies, particularly Marcus Aurelius. I read these pieces diligently from January 1st to December 31st, and they changed how I saw the world. Stoicism holds that you can only control what is in your control, and there's no point in worrying about anything else. One of the toxic effects of imposter syndrome is the constant comparison with others and their achievements. Stopping being concerned about what other people have achieved and concentrating on what you can and have achieved seems like the perfect anecdote. So be responsible for your actions but not those of others. Concentrate on yours.

I started using a Self Journal around the same time to

organise my day and be more productive. I'm not sure it achieved that goal, but it required me to write three things for which I was grateful in the morning and three in the evening. I've always been a "cup half-full" person, so I'm possibly more predisposed to a gratitude practice. It was hard at first, but the more I did it, the easier it became. I don't need to write things down anymore; they just are. Gratitude made me concentrate on what I have, not what I don't.

I still suffer from imposter syndrome and always will. It manifests itself in subtle ways now, but it's always manageable. I was looking at Linkedin recently for prospects to target. I'm first-level connected to heads of marketing at Red Bull and Ferrari. As much as part of me would love to work with brands like that, it's not going to happen. I had a moment of panic, thinking I was entirely out of my depth with them. But who said I had to target them? No one, so I won't. That's one way to deal with it.

My imposter syndrome makes me procrastinate. This book may have taken considerably less time to write were it not for that. The key to controlling the condition is to recognise it. It doesn't like being called out and prefers operating in the shadows where no one can see it. By calling it out, you give it a form that puts you in charge. "By all means, exist", you can say. "but sit in the corner and shut up; I don't want to hear a peep from you." Generally, it does what it's told.

Imposter syndrome is often a sign of growth. It means you are putting yourself in uncomfortable positions. In his book *Mastering Fear—A Navy Seal's Guide*, Brandon Webb describes how Navy Seals are trained. They learn to face every possible scenario; the last thing they need is to be in a life-threatening situation where they don't know what to do. So they cover everything. They have no truck with the term "comfort zone" because stepping out of it implies pain. Their approach is to expand their "zone of competence", whereby there are no surprises and no pain. I can't help but agree with them. So when I do something new, it's an experience. It makes it enjoyable. And as I love learning new things, it's a painless experience.

I'll let Neil Gaiman have the last word. "Some years ago, I was lucky enough to be invited to a gathering of great and good people: artists and scientists, writers and discoverers. And at any moment, they would realise that I didn't qualify to be there among these people who had really done things.

On my second or third night there, I was standing at the back of the hall while a musical entertainment happened, and I started talking to a very nice, polite, elderly gentleman about several things, including our shared first name. And then he pointed to the hall of people, and said words to the effect of, "I just look at all these people, and I think, what the heck am I doing here? They've made amazing things. I just went where I was sent." The Neil in question was Neil Armstrong. There is clearly hope for us all.

Thinking it has to be perfect

Like it or not, caring about what other people think is one of those things that makes us human and keeps us alive. A study by University College London and Aarhus University in Denmark found that the area of our brains associated with reward is more active when others agree with and support our opinions.

That's also how echo chambers work. We fill them with people whose opinions we agree with so we never get challenged and never have to justify them. However nauseous they may be, we don't want to feel excluded from the group. The herd mentality enables us to entertain our darkest thoughts. We seek the approval of our peers as part of our desire to survive. The more we stick together, the less we stand out.

Luckily, most of our peers aren't dicks, and it doesn't get that bad. But we still fear what other people think. At its worst, it can transform into debilitating fear so bad it has a name, "allodoxaphobia." It can affect your ability to do basic tasks and make decisions. It also affects how you communicate, how you feel you can be yourself and ultimately, the image you portray.

The potential judgement of other people has often crippled me. But the reality is everyone can't like you for the simple reason that you don't like everyone. Here is not the place to go into the dark psychological reasons, but people-pleasers have always had trouble with the judgement of others.

Living up to other people's expectations is exhausting. As an exercise, I searched "are you a people pleaser" online and I ticked all the boxes. And I mean all of them—pretending to agree with people, feeling responsible for how other people think, apologising all the time, not being able to say no or feeling uncomfortable whenever anyone is angry with me.

Conformity is a human trait. As Robert Cialdini pointed out, we trust people who share our views, pay us compliments, and with whom we share a common cause. We look for areas of similarity in others. Just look at the headlines on any magazine stand or in any newspaper.

- Ten things you should watch on Netflix
- Clothes you shouldn't wear after fifty
- Lose your gut!
- All the trends to shop now
- Dress like a boss

Newspapers, magazines and social media are full of people judging others for their life choices. People tell us to "fit in" and not stand out. From an early age, the playground teaches us that transgressing that rule is fraught with danger. So we mirror the behaviours and attitudes of our peers early on and reject people or perspectives that don't fit in.

In 1951, Soloman Asch carried out an experiment that proved that people are guided by their confirmation bias and make wrong choices just to follow what everyone else is doing.

Fifty students were broken into groups of 8 and asked a series of questions. However, 7 of them already knew the answers that were expected. The eighth provided the same one, whether it was right or not.

People went against all the evidence and their better judgement and agreed with other people's choices so that they didn't have to stand out. Group mentality confirmed that the majority opinion was the right one. But anyone who has ever made a difference in the world has done so... by not fitting in, have they not?

They are those that Steve Jobs once called "the crazy ones." The now iconic ads for the Think Different campaign featured well-known conformists like Richard Branson, who lives by "Screw it, let's do it", whatever other people think, Martha Graham, whose style reshaped American dance and is taught worldwide to this day and Mahatma Gandhi, who lead an independence movement and stood up to the might of the soon to crumble British Empire.

So, where does that leave us? Stuck in limbo between a natural human desire to be part of the crowd and what we know to be a business necessity to stand out from it. That's interesting, isn't it? And therein lies the key problem most of us face.

While trying to stand out, many businesses unconsciously want to be the same as everyone else because they're afraid of being mocked by their peers, industry, and even their customers. Competitors will say mean things to them, but above all, they're scared they might offend someone.

The reasons may be deep-rooted fears in our culture, parents, or previous business experience, but none need to be true. The greatest businesses will offend or upset someone at one stage or another. And the problem with not wanting to offend anyone is that you end up appealing to no one. You can't appeal to everyone; many have tried and floundered. Your story and your beliefs will be your secret weapon.

I remember the first Body Shop set up in Brighton in the late 70s from my student days. Back then, the name invoked more car bodies than human ones. It was in Kensington Gardens between two funeral directors and I remember the fragrant smell and the handwritten product labels when taken in there by my girlfriend at the time.

But what made the business stand out more than anything? Its refusal to test on animals. That may seem quite normal to us, but in 1976, according to some, Anita Roddick was a maverick, a crackpot. Part of the "loony left" radical fringe that inhabited the back streets of Brighton plotting (a very tabloid word) to undermine our society. It was most cool to go shopping there.

When Apple took a stand against anti-LGBT legislation under consideration in onetime Vice-President Pence's North Carolina, it had no direct impact on its business. Still, it recognised that customers care about what they sell and what they stand for.

You don't need to be big to have principles. I have a client who runs a fledgling property management company which has pledged to donate a percentage of his profits to local charities as part of this belief that businesses do not exist in a vacuum and are part of the wider society. Some will love him for it, and some will accuse him of posturing and that so-called insult so beloved of the Right, virtue-signalling. He doesn't care. There's a thin line between being a maverick, a change-maker, and a dick. The solution is to have something you stand for. Having a purpose is not just for big businesses. The Body Shop was a micro-business when it started, and it has primarily held onto its principles over the years as it has grown into a massive institution owned by an even more massive group.

The stories we tell ourselves

One problem I have looking back on my life is wondering whether any of the events occurred. I hate to tell you, but we are terrible witnesses to our lives. Our memories lie to us all the time.

I'm part of the generation who watched *Star Trek* reruns in the early 70s when the franchise was gaining momentum but wasn't yet the "Original Series" it was to become. It was required for early evening viewing. I've always thought it went out on Saturday night, but in fact, it was a midweek affair on a Tuesday. Saturday evening was the preserve of *Doctor Who, The Wonderful World of Disney* or *The Generation Game* in the early 70s.

I have memories of watching Kirk, Spock, et al. sitting in a small sky blue-coloured rattan cane chair at home in the living room with my parents as clear as day, even as I write this fifty years later. Except I was 14 in 1972 and a biggish lad. That little blue chair was one of those small ones given to three or four-year-olds so they could feel part of the family. There is no way I could have been sitting in it then.

When I was six years old. I sat in school assembly with all the other kids cross-legged on the floor—apart from me. I did it in a half-assed way, sprawling over the place and probably invading at least one of my neighbours' spaces. It hurt a bit because it wasn't very natural for me. Or so I thought. I spent my life telling myself I had no balance and wasn't flexible. Then I started yoga recently because I was concerned that, getting older, I wouldn't be able to move around as easily as I used to. And you know what? I can cross my legs just fine. Sitting with a straight back is fine too, if I make myself do it. And I can even stand on my left leg for a bit. The right one, though, is more of a work in progress.

Somewhere about 1972 or 1973, I found myself at Craven Cottage, Fulham. It was one of the first football games I went to on my own. They hadn't yet built the stand that now protects supporters in the then terraces from the icy winds that used to swirl around the ground, giving fans a distinct impression of being in the Arctic.

My memory is that I went to two games. One against Brighton on 27th January 1973 when they won 5-1. The record books on Wikipedia record the game just fine. The second is a mystery. I'm sure they played Arsenal around the same time, although I can't remember the score. Peter Marinello—the new George Best—was part of the Arsenal team. I can remember him coming down the left wing at pace. There is absolutely no public record of that game. Arsenal and Fulham weren't in the same division and didn't have a league game between 1968 and 2001. I was 9 in 1968; I doubt I was there. Peter Marinello certainly wasn't.

If those events aren't strange enough, there are also things I thought couldn't have happened but did. My earliest memory is the birth of my little brother when I was 3. I remember coming home from the hospital in the car. Children didn't get to see inside a hospital ward in 1961 unless it was in a bed, as I discovered later. So I didn't get to see the baby until we were in the car on the way home.

I remember sitting in the back seat of my grandmother's pre-1960 VW Beetle with mechanical direction indicators rather than lights with my baby brother, only a few days old, on my lap. The car was moving. All this happened in the days before seat belts at the front of the car, let alone the back. It didn't seem to bother my grandmother or my mother in the slightest. I can only presume my over-cautious father wasn't there.

I've long thought entrusting a three-year-old on the back seat of a VW Beetle with a newborn was nuts and couldn't have happened. But years later, my mother confirmed it did. Health and safety legislation exists now for a reason.

These stories come from the narratives I have in my head. Back in the very early times, the group's Alpha male cried "danger" or "food", and the others followed because he'd created a narrative in their heads. He'd managed to persuade them of the best thing to do. They'd be safer or no longer hungry if they followed him. They'd be better people.

Later, when the group got too big for the alpha male to control, other stories were created to keep it together. They built communities as they roamed, looking for food and shelter. They developed languages that would keep them out of danger and provide sustenance. When they felt safe and well-fed, they started forming groups within groups powered by gossip and telling stories about other groups. That's where our stories are born; they control our lives. We all do it.

Life as we know it is a mess, a series of random events thrown together without regard for logic, sense or justice. And we're expected to deal with it. Journalist Joan Didion's collection of essays, *The White Album*, starts with: "We tell ourselves stories to live." We create stories to give our lives meaning and however good, bad or indifferent they are, we all create internal narratives. They give us structure and meaning without which we'd go through our lives adrift and rudderless.

We invent stories to make sense of it all. It's of little import whether they're true or not; our lives would make no sense otherwise. Our memories would be meaningless. There would be no order where sense and nonsense have equal value.

There's an important difference between fact and truth. Facts are immovable; we did land on the moon—tell Buzz Aldrin otherwise and he'll bop you on the nose. The Earth is not flat and is over 6,000 years old. We can prove it. Paul McCartney didn't die in 1967, and there is no lookalike. Just think of the career his lookalike has had since then. I could go on with the even more bonkers conspiracy theories like Saddam Hussein's Stargate or the Queen being a cannibal.

But truth, however, is a moving object. It varies from one person to the next. Our truth is what helps us get through life.

I'm not creative

One of the great myths is that some people are born creative, others are not. I've lost count over the years of the number of people who, when I tell them I'm a writer, say, "oh, I'm not creative." It's almost a Pavlovian response.

Then the same people will move on to the "Oh; you're so lucky to be able to write." Well, yes, I am. Or I'm lucky enough to know that anyone can write. I was terrible when I started, but I practised.

Let's deal with the "I'm not creative" myth right now. There is a ton of research to say that this is hokum. George Land conducted the first study into this over fifty years ago, in 1968. He gave 1600 four- and five-year-old children tests designed for candidates for NASA. He tested them again five and ten years later and compared the scores with adults who took the tests simultaneously. 98% of the 5-year-olds tested were in the genius stage of imagination; only 30% of the 10-year-olds and 12% of 15-year-olds were still there. Only 2% of the 280,000 adults tested were still in that genius stage by the age of 31.

He found that there are two types of thinking, divergent, which encourages imagination and convergent, where we make judgements and criticise. The studies found that as we educate our children and adults, we simultaneously teach them both types of thinking, not unlike Carol Dwek's fixed and growth mindsets, but the convergent methods win in the end because creative people who stand out are feared.

So when we start coming up with new ideas as adults, what we mostly learned in school kicks in, and the criticisms arrive. "We've done that before", "We've never done that", "That's crazy", "It'll cost too much," "We're sensible adults" or the parent who says, "don't be stupid"

The five-year-old in us gets banished. However, that kid never went away; the potential for imagination gets pushed to the back of our brains. It's something we exercise every day when we dream. We've all heard a parent telling their child not to be silly when they come up with an imaginary idea. That's a terrible thing to say. It's perhaps time to tap into that child.

The Greeks and Romans thought creativity was a spirit that lived outside the body. Daemons or genii visited you and bestowed moments of creativity on you. On the days when we didn't feel inspired, they'd obviously taken a day off and would come back later. The beauty of this intellectual construct was that it took all the guilt away because we weren't in control of our creativity. We couldn't call ourselves lazy or worthless; it was just that the genius, or the muse wasn't doing the daily rounds. The downside was that we couldn't take credit for great work.

The Renaissance rejected that idea, and the blame for the lack of inspiration shifted towards us. We now see genius as a reflection of inherent ability rather than a spiritual visitation. Still, the idea of creative inspiration just hitting us persists, as does the guilt that comes with it when it fails to turn up.

People ride with an image of the wild, temperamental artist in his ivory tower who spends his days creating things of such imponderable depth that none of us mere mortals could ever understand them. Things plop out of their brains, and they process them in ways that are not available to us—they write, they draw, and they paint all the time. If only.

Yet creativity is not about being able to draw, paint or even write. Those are the tools we use to be creative. Real creativity comes with the generation of ideas. And we all have those. Ideas are the building blocks of creativity; without them, we are nothing.

The so-called division between creatives and non-creatives is a false one. Everyone in business, self-employment or working for the Man, has ideas. So it's impossible not to be creative, especially when we get back in touch with that 5-year-old.

Early humans weren't particularly well suited to survive. They couldn't run very fast, had no fur, and couldn't fly. Neither could they swim underwater for any length of time. So how the hell did they survive and, indeed, thrive over all the other animals kicking around at the time? Because they had brains and solved problems creatively.

They used sticks to ward off sabre-toothed tiger-sized dangers, built things to protect themselves, made clothes and weapons, built shelters when they realised they didn't have to live in caves and made the first sharpened stone tools.

Once they acquired survival, they moved on with more sophisticated clothing, more advanced shelter and body paint to identify themselves—that was the beginning of fashion. They built taller buildings and more elaborate shelters, they built cathedrals, the Sistine Chapel and went to the Moon.

The desire to grow our businesses and, indeed, grow as individuals is a basic human need. With no ideas, you wouldn't get very far.

So how do we come up with them? There are plenty of systems for coming up with ideas, but what do you do then? You write them down. Time management guru David Allen says, "Our brains are for having ideas, not storing them"

James Webb Young was a successful advertising man working on Madison Avenue in New York in the 1930s. One day, one of his clients asked him how he got his ideas. He wrote his response in a book published in 1939, "A Technique for Producing Ideas" It's not very long, only 48 pages, but he packed more goodness into those pages than many a weighty tome produced since then, and it encapsulates all you need to know about getting started with idea generation.

You probably should read it, but for now I'll summarise it here.

Step One: Gather the raw materials

Don't sit around waiting for inspiration to strike. It won't. Inspiration has to be fed, so be curious.

In practical terms, this means when you are faced with a practical problem, gather all the elements of that problem around you. Use post-it notes, a whiteboard, a legal pad or

Evernote, whatever is your weapon of choice. Know a lot about your subject, but also look at things all around you.

Step Two: Digest (masticate)

Stand back and throw all your material in a different light. Connect the dots (or not)

"Creativity is just connecting things" Steve Jobs

Step Three: Don't think

Let your thoughts roam, sleep on them. Walk away. Do something else that stimulates your imagination. Your brain is a muscle, and you have your best moments of inspiration in the shower.

Step Four: Eureka!

Ideas will come from nowhere; that's when you need a notebook handy.

Capture, or it'll be gone.

Step Five: Bring the idea into reality. Put it out to the test. Subject it to criticism. Have many ideas.

"It is better to have enough ideas for some of them to be wrong than to always be right by having no ideas at all"

Edward de Bono.

Creativity is central to us as business owners and also to us telling our stories. So is that 5-year-old who still lies within you, however old, wisened and grumpy you may feel? We are all creative; the trouble is that the adults in the room sometimes take up too much space.

Success is a moving object

Sometimes I think I'm having a good day when I have little wins like getting a new client, understanding a new thing or just when someone says something nice to me. Today is a good day just because I resisted the temptation to say something bad about myself in that sentence. I count that as a win for positive self-talk.

Self-doubt is good because it's a sign of humility. Failing is fine because it's the only way we get good at things. That's why people always say that if babies gave up every time they tried to walk and fell flat on their arses, we'd all be shuffling around on our backsides now. It's trite and reductive, but it's also true. We must get comfortable with being bad at things before we get good. That's as much part of our story as all the success. The British like imperfection more than anyone else; the story of the plucky loser runs deep in our culture. Yet, it makes the successes when they occur even sweeter.

You can't get rid of fear either; it's energy and trying to beat it head-on only makes it stronger. You can turn it into positive energy as long as it doesn't get in the way. Just noticing it and welcoming it disarms it. It has nowhere to go, so it slinks off and bothers someone else.

The imposter gremlins are the same. They'll beat you to a pulp if you let them. But we all get it; just ask Neil Armstrong.

All those stories we tell ourselves are largely just that, stories. We can carry narratives around in our heads for years. I thought I was the ugly duckling who would never amount to anything because of something a 13-year-old girl I found stunningly attractive said to me. She crushed me. Of course, it was all tosh; I've amounted to quite a lot and am improving daily. Ironically, I became friends with that 13-year-old when we were 17 and 18—no romance was involved—that's what growing up does for you.

You have everything in you, and you can't control the reactions of others. Our failures improve us, and those stories may not be true. You are creative, and you are capable. And you are responsible for what happens next.

Chapter 7

Things To Expect When You Run A Business

The exciting adventure of running a business

I t has to be said that running your own business is a gift. While my experience has sometimes been challenging, I'm not suited to working for someone else. I'm a terrible employee. Working for myself is the best thing I've ever done, and there was never any going back.

Television and fiction do an excellent job of glorifying running a business and misrepresenting it at the same time. If you watched "reality" programmes like The Apprentice or even Dragon's Den/Shark Tank or fiction like Billions or Succession, you'd think that's what business is like. All power suits, glamour and dirty deeds. I may have seen the odd underhand deal from time to time, but that's not a representation of business I recognise.

According to the Small Business Administration in 2020, there were over 31 million small businesses in the US in 2020. UK Government figures say there are 5.5 million. That's a lot of people trying to make a living outside a corporate structure that provides everything for you. In corporate life, the only time you might ever come across accountants, sales and marketing or anyone in production was at the office party. Now, when you start, at least, you have to do it all. It's not for everyone; the ride can get bumpy.

People will say they do it to have more free time and to choose when they work, to be in control and make all the decisions, and of course, to make a ton of money. And they're right. But the reality is often far less glamorous. Running a business means you'll be making decisions all the time. If you're not careful, that can lead to decision paralysis that is so bad nothing ever gets done. Running a business involves drudgery. It means turning up every day to do things you don't want or don't like to do. It means periods of self-doubt. There will be questions. You'll ask yourself if you should have left that cushy corporate job. Did you behave in the right way with that client? Where is the next client going to come from?

It means spinning plates juggling the responsibilities of home and work when everyone wants stuff straight away. There will be days when you get tired and oversleep, miss a client call and have to apologise profusely. There will be days when you'll mess up with something. There will be days when you'll want to give up and live on a desert island on the other side of the world. It means managing your diary down to the millimetre just to keep on top of things. The self-doubt and the stress can be crippling if you let them. I'm not selling it well, am I?

However, there are no office politics to deal with. There are no crappy bosses who think they're still in the military and all they have to do is snap their fingers for you to do something or think it's alright to call you at the weekend when you're having lunch with the in-laws. It means that the things you accomplish are your wins; you don't need to share them with anyone. It means a sense of achievement you could never get when working for someone else. It's yours, all yours.

Disclaimer: all these may or may not have happened to my friends or me. My lips are sealed. Running a business is rather like life. Ups and downs, you take the rough with the smooth; there's no model to adhere to. That would be too easy.

I only have my experience and that of the people I've spoken to go by, but there are universal things you can expect when you run a business, and you can draw on them for your story because everything is a story.

Expect the unexpected

"Everyone Has a Plan Until They Get Punched in the Mouth"

Often falsely attributed to Mike Tyson—it's an adaptation of a quote by a nineteenth-century German Field-Marshal named Moltke the Elder, who said, "No plan of operations extends with certainty beyond the first encounter with the enemy's main strength"—the principle is the same.

You can make all the plans you like, but only when you start putting them into action do they really take shape. It's rather like when you learn to drive; the learning starts when you get your licence.

The world has thrown a lot at us in the last two or three years and continues to do so. Your business can get thrown about by all kinds of bumps in the road; the important part is how you tell these stories and use them in your business.

Bumps in the road will always happen; that's life. But

they're also an opportunity if we want to make them so. We are responsible for what happens next.

There may be a possibly toxic relationship between late-night alcohol and just jumping on the Internet, I couldn't possibly confirm.

One Saturday night in November 2002, I may have had one sherbert too many. I was living alone and watching late-night TV. It was already Sunday when I fired up the Internet with that old bippity bop dial-up sound and took a look at Friends Reunited, a now-defunct site that brought together old school friends from the 60s, 70s and 80s.

I'd already had conversations with one or two old classmates, but they didn't go any further. We were 30 years older and we had very little in common anymore. But then I saw one name that stopped me in my tracks. Janice Gough.

I met her when I was 14; she was still 12. I'm almost two years older than her, so although we were born a mile apart and were at the same school, we didn't know each other. I have to pinch myself sometimes when I remember that.

We met on a school trip to Paris in 1973 and things went on from there. She was 13 by the time we "went out" together, and we continued to frequent each other for the next three or four years. But then life took over; she left school, went to work and hooked up with my "best friend" at the time. I eventually made it to university, and, apart from an aborted attempt at going out together a couple of years later, our paths separated.

But we never really forgot. There must've been something lurking in the back of our minds. My heart was racing when I saw her name, and I knew I might never contact her if I didn't do so there and then. I was terrified of how she might answer if she answered at all. I wasn't looking forward to the rejection but, in a way, expecting it.

This was when I was going to find out what had happened in the intervening twenty-five years. I knew she had three kids because my mother was friends with her then husband's mother. The twist in that particular tale is that I've known her (ex-) husband since we were both nine—longer than I've known her. I thought she'd ridden off into the sunset for a happy and probably successful life. I still thought she was out of my league.

She answered, and it turns out that by 2002 we were ripe for a reunion. And it was quick. We had none of the "getting to know you" stuff that other people have when they first meet, nor the relationship-building stuff; we were filling in the gaps.

She told me she thought we had unfinished business, and she was right. Whatever fears I had didn't extend beyond the first encounter. We started emailing in November 2002, saw each other in April 2003, and by July, we were living together. We got married a little more than a year later. I cried when she walked into the room at the ceremony. There had been a lot of pent up emotion.

You never know what is going to happen. There's always something around the corner that could be good or bad, but it's most likely unexpected. I moved back from Brittany, thinking I could be close to her so we could see each other more often, but she said we should live together. So we tried a 6-month experiment. I guess getting married was proof that it worked.

I changed countries but didn't necessarily change cultures. I still have my feet firmly planted between the two. I became a better translator and writer though, because I lived in the culture and the language I was working in.

It edged out the bad practices I'd gotten myself into in my mother tongue and stopped me from drifting from one to the other. I said some strange things when I came back, like going "under the shower" and not in it. You know what it means, but it ain't right. To this day, I say "Aie" and not "Ouch" when I whack myself by accident. I may have gone a little too native, but perhaps late-night boozing and the Internet aren't necessarily a bad combination.

Kenda MacDonald has had an unconventional journey into digital marketing via South Africa, forensic psychology and the Metropolitan Police. In fact, if it hadn't been for the Met, she might not have been in marketing at all. Kenda had a dream; she wanted to be a forensic psychologist and got the opportunity to move from her native South Africa and train with the British police force in London. It was the perfect deal; her training would be funded, and she would live in barracks with no student debt.

Except she hadn't reckoned on having to naturalise before being able to work for the Metropolitan Police. A process that was going to take five years. So she'd upped sticks and moved her entire life to London only to find that she'd have to wait an eternity for the crock of gold she'd been expecting when she arrived.

She had her back up against the wall. So she lived with her mother and did temp jobs just to pay the bills before getting into Birkbeck University and restarting the career path she'd always wanted to follow. Fortunately, Birbeck's classes take place in the evenings. She had time during the day to continue to earn her keep. She got a job with a marketing agency that, on her first day, asked her to use a complicated programme to build an email marketing campaign. The clients had been making angry phone calls when they couldn't work out how to use the software they used, and her boss wanted her to fail just like them.

With a combination of YouTube videos and search engines,

she worked it out and, within eight months, was building his campaigns and running the implementation side of the business. It was a beautiful coincidence to be learning about marketing at the same time as learning about how the brain works. While she kept trying to bring behaviour into her work, her boss kept pushing her back, showing no interest in trying new things.

When that business failed, the logical next step was to do it herself. It just made sense for Kenda to do marketing in ways that made the brain happy. After so much pushback and insistence from her boss on doing things in ways that didn't work, she finally had the opportunity to start applying the findings of forensic psychology to marketing.

Kenda's approach is science-based, and there's an undercurrent of psychology behind everything she does. And most of the time, the process worked. When it didn't, she tried to figure out why because that's what empirical scientists do. They get results because they work, "... not because a random guru on the Internet says they should do it"

She was initially shy about telling people why she does what she does. Then, a couple of years in, then realised it might be an idea to start shouting about it. People were interested and excited. And the more people she told about it, the more people told her to write it down.

Kenda didn't finish her degree, the business needed to generate more money to pay for the fees for the final exams, and after two and a half years of working for herself, she felt like she was floundering.

Her original career path had given her a sense of purpose. She was good at technology, science and maths and could have become a doctor or a surgeon. But she chose forensic psychology and pathology because it was all she'd ever wanted to do. It was one of "those weird things that we have as a child ... I wanted to make the world a better place ... I would be effectively fixing society's problems."

She realised she wouldn't be fixing problems by going into forensics; she'd just be picking up the pieces. "Criminal psychology looks sexy on TV shows, but in real life, it's tough. It's opening a window on some of the worst things people can do to each other." So she had nothing; the sense of purpose was gone.

She started with a course but quickly realised she was created a monster that was fast getting out of control. It would be difficult to sell and even more difficult to complete.

She'd been working with our mutual friend Vicky Quinn Fraser who suggested she turn it into a book. Initially, imposter syndrome kicked in again. But she thought she'd never be able to do that, but she'd spent four years researching it and pulling things together. Reading other people's books convinced her she could do better. She's an expert.

"What was really exciting was no longer feeling like I had gone off the rails and not feeling like I'd ruined my life coming to the UK. After all, that very clearly defined academic career path was not something I'd taken. And I went on this really freakin' crazy journey for years doing all sorts of weird stuff. And suddenly, it all made sense. Everything came together. I realised that was what I wanted to do. I wanted to write, and I wanted to talk about things. And I wanted to teach people to be better with their businesses and better for their consumers. And things started to come together. And I felt like I had a purpose, and I hadn't just totally fucked up my life." She was doing what she originally wanted to do but in a slightly different way.

Between finishing the book and starting to speak publicly,

there was a wobble. She was making money to survive, but it was a struggle. She could make a lot of money working with large, corporate clients, but she realised that if she worked with smaller, passionate businesses—she's fussy about who she works with—who are making the world a better place through what they're doing she could have a ripple effect. She would make the world better for her client, who would make the world better for all their clients and so on.

"That's all I care about. I care about making the world better. And I can do it this way by helping businesses get their messages out, especially working with ethical companies. It's why book number two will be about conscious consumerism and the fact that consumers are smart. I'm going to teach people how cognitive bias works, how to make people aware of it, and how, when you do that, how much better their marketing is by being good to your audience, ethical, moral, and sustainable. Not just from a green perspective but from a human perspective. That is better for people in general, but it's also more profitable.

The journey has been rocky, with several bumps along the way, but Kenda has found her path. The bumps that come along are largely unforeseeable, but every so often, the damage caused by these hiccups is self-inflicted. We make the wrong decision, and things can go wrong. Or right. It all depends on how you look at it.

Growth is a process, not a goal

By any stretch of the imagination, Joanna Wiebe is successful. She started Copy Hackers with information products on copywriting and as a vehicle for her writing output in 2011.

Now, it's one of the world's largest educational resources for copywriters.

She's self-deprecating about it, almost embarrassed at her success and accredits a lot of it to being in the right place at the right time. While that may be true, she still had to take the opportunities presented to her and Joanna has done that in spades. There was no master plan when she started; she fell into Copy Hackers almost accidentally. And quite naturally.

She'd always played with Lego when she was young, "... before Lego got really cool. It was the 90s, and I think a lot of people who go into business actually started playing Lego. I look back at it and think I'm a builder. I like building things. I like making things. I never built anything in Lego and then put it on the shelf. I built it. And then I knocked it apart. And I built it again, in a different way, doing something different. I never had kits where I had a book to follow. You just liked bringing something neat to life. And in your head, it was incredible. And your parents looked at it (and said), 'that's just that's another little red house, Joanna; stop building so many red houses."

She built Copy Hackers like that based on the principles of Eric Ries's *The Lean Startup*. She constantly innovated by making things and breaking them when they stopped working. The story goes that she prepared an "I quit" email one day in her job at Intuit when she was particularly dissatisfied with her boss. We've all done that in our time, and the wise thing to do would have been to sleep on it and delete it the next day. Jo was going to do just that. Except that rather than hitting the Save button, she hit the Send button. She'd committed herself. Copy Hackers started as she meant to go on.

She'd already built a website in Canada with a few friends that ranked realtors in a variety of ways. It took off and got good traction in the days before the Internet gave you ratings for everything and everyone. The site must have ruffled a few feathers because the Canadian Realtors Association found out about it and required her to take it down. It was a fun project and only ever intended as such, but it was a proof of concept and a trial run. Jo could build something more than Lego houses and make it a success.

She says that writing is the only thing she's ever been good at and couldn't imagine doing anything else—apart from running a coffee shop because she loves coffee. That's all she needed to give her greater confidence in her ability than anyone else I've talked to for this book. Even though her first interaction with the world of writing was watching a 90s TV show that may have been with Kirstie Alley—she was a brunette and thought she recognised her from Cheers—as a struggling writer. Her takeaway at the time was that she shouldn't become a writer because they struggle. It didn't stop her in the end.

She helped a business owner on Y Combinator's Hacker News with a copy critique who reported later that he "received a professional, detailed deck of tons of invaluable well thought out feedback. It must have taken her an entire afternoon." That resulted in a deluge of requests, far more than she could reasonably handle. On the one hand, that was bad because she couldn't help everyone, but it was good because it proved that people wanted what she was offering. Hacker News and Y Combinator were then, as now, deeply involved in the start-up world and the Lean Startup movement was the perfect vehicle if she found one of her ideas didn't work. Just like the Lego bricks.

She wrote a series of PDFs about copywriting and made about $20,000 from them in just a couple of days. She was onto something. Dharmesh Shah, the founder of HubSpot, was one of the first to buy. "That was cool", "A good feeling", she said. That's something of an understatement. She says that when you're in business, you have lots of goals, and sometimes, the things that may be "cool accomplishments" are easy to forget when you have so many things on the go. Sometimes you have to sit back and take stock and appreciate when things are going well.

When she split from her business partner and took complete control of Copy Hackers, she knew it was time to take things seriously. She started looking at it as a real business, making plans and hiring the right people. That was when Copy School, the flagship program that is the core of everything Copy Hackers does, started to kick in.

When Copy Hackers started, there were no masterminds to join or anything that taught writers how to be freelancers. There were books to teach copywriting skills, such as Luke Sullivan's *Hey Whipple Squeeze* or the much older but nevertheless classic *Breakthrough Advertising* by Gene Schwartz. But these were intimidating for beginner copywriters —*Breakthrough Advertising* was out of print, and copies sold for getting on for $900 online—so there was a clear need for something else.

Copy Hackers has been built on trial and error. Ideas were tried, adapted and dropped if they didn't work. The original courses are no longer available, but Copy School is now a platform that includes everything and anything any aspiring or even accomplished one could ever want or need.

She faces problems, obviously. Being a builder means she gets distracted by shiny objects constantly. She spends a lot of time wondering whether she's focused on the right things, but she's built a business over the years through constant iteration, so having many things on the go is to be expected. She's always looking at new things but is still in lean start-up mode. If something doesn't make it through the early experimental stage, it goes. If it does, it gets her full attention and gets all the way to market. Shiny object syndrome implies starting things and getting distracted because something new comes along. That's not quite Jo; she has a process for jettisoning things that don't work.

She's also aware that she has a great team in place currently but is challenged every time she has to grow it. "I cannot complain enough about the challenges of hiring the right people", she says. Finding people who blend into a team that works and help move the business forward is always a challenge.

And then there's the comparison demon. It's easy to look at what businesses are doing and wonder if you could do it too. Many have lost their way doing that and moving away from their core purpose. Copy Hackers is a training company; it has even ditched its copywriting agency to concentrate on what it does best. The decision had to be made. Again.

I asked her whether Copy Hackers could survive without her. She's the public face of the "brand" and probably always will be because it's her baby. But it is also a team, and once you get past the gate, you realise there are plenty of others in the business. She still loves it.

Frustratingly for us mortals, she's never had any doubts about what she does. The lean start-up culture means guilt-free failure is hard-wired into it. It's part of a process where something is started, she runs with it for a while, and if it doesn't work, she moves on to the next thing. She's currently looking at copywriting boot camps, like coding boot camps, where aspiring copywriters will be taught everything about the craft from A to Z in a short intensive period. For now, it will be online, but ultimately the aim is to hold them in a classroom situation. Hardcore.

She has no self-doubt, much to the surprise of some of her team, but it's all she's ever done. Everything comes back to building Lego houses and taking them down again until she gets it right.

Expect to be vulnerable

When Brené Brown stood up on the stage at TEDx in Houston in 2010 to talk about the power of vulnerability, she had no idea what she was about to unleash.

She says that after the initial talk, she had the "worst vulnerability hangover ever" and was ashamed that 500 or 600 people had seen it. YouTube was planning to release it, and she feared it might get a couple thousand views. If that were the case, "my life will end." She had no contingency for four million. And that was in 2012; she's had many more views since then.

In the right hands, vulnerability is a potent tool to show leadership and compassion, especially in times of crisis. It seems to be everywhere these days, but what is it?

Google "what is vulnerability", and most results will be dictionary definitions or military strategies. Very few will cover emotional vulnerability.

Brené Brown describes it as "... the birthplace of love, belonging, joy, courage, empathy, and creativity. It is the source of hope, empathy, accountability, and authenticity. If we want greater clarity in our purpose or deeper and more meaningful spiritual lives, vulnerability is the path." It is not weakness; it's an act of courage.

Starting a business is an act of vulnerability. As Seth Godin says, it's the process of saying, "hey, I made this; I hope you like it." I know many copywriters who take a deep breath every time they send something out, a fight to the death between imposter syndrome and vulnerability raging in their heads.

We're plagued with thoughts of "what if the client doesn't like it?" or "What if someone does it better?" Vulnerability is where creators and innovators go to present their work; it's the place for new ideas .. the birthplace of innovation, creativity and change"

The most important and scary place to be vulnerable is in marketing and telling a story as part of it. What do you put in? What do you leave out?

Former *This American Life* producer Alex Blumberg started his own podcast production company with a partner and decided to document it with ... a podcast. He showed the early months, then a couple of years of the development of the business with all the botched attempts at raising investor cash, the late-night soul searching with his wife and his imposter syndrome, wondering whether he was doing the right thing. I listened to every episode walking the dog at night. It really is warts and all but compelling at the same time.

The result is endearing; Blumberg portrayed himself as a real person with hopes and fears without over-sharing. By being open, he told an origin story, an ongoing one with potentially no end. It was relatable and carried all the emotions that business owners can identify with at all stages of the journey, not just the setbacks.

The danger with being vulnerable in this manner is that there are no gatekeepers, and anyone can say anything because it's "free speech." There's no line between "I run a business" and "I am a brand." The lack of a filter can lead to over-sharing and self-indulgence.

We'll leave aside the Instagram influencers who are famous for being famous and torpedoed themselves in a couple of ill-judged videos. Your audience is not your support system if you're a business. It's not a good look.

There is a difference between being vulnerable and over-sharing in a world without gatekeepers. Some business owners can lose a sense of boundaries.

Authenticity is about being brave enough to be yourself and genuine enough to live according to your values. Authentic means what you say and do must align with what you believe. We used to call it "walking the walk and talking the talk."

Some think "being honest" or "saying it how it is" is somehow authentic. There are places and times when this view has been somewhat distorted. More often than not, it's just being obnoxious.

Sharing a mistake, however painful, so that others may learn is vulnerable and an act of courage. If you want pity, that's over-sharing and will ruin your reputation. Putting personal information out to make people think you are granting them intimacy will do you no good either.

Sometimes, vulnerable leadership goes so wrong it resembles a badly scripted TV movie. The very public implosion of Miki Agrawal, CEO of the period-proof underwear brand THINX, is a case in point. For example, the "openness" she embodied, Face Timing from the toilet, made many of her employees rather uncomfortable. There were allegations of misdemeanours mainly relating to a lack of adequate HR provisions or policy that were later withdrawn. Still, as Agrawal said on Medium later, "I did not think it was inappropriate at the time, especially since we had such an open and friendly culture, but I certainly learned that it could be seen that way."

Vulnerability starts to tip into oversharing and basic dickheadidness once the emphasis is more on the leader than the team, who will be looking for guidance and not to guide. That's not the team's job.

The things that make us vulnerable are difficult to talk about while they are going on. A public meltdown will invariably undermine your credibility as a business and possibly as a person. It will also put off your clients and potential audience. In the middle of a crisis, it's not their role to be your therapist or saviour. You can't have an objective view. No one wants to see you in the middle of a meltdown.

But a public showing of strength and honesty can make you sound human. It won't necessarily get you sales, but it will do your reputation no harm at all.

On being wrong

I was six, perhaps seven, and a bunch of young boys were in the toilets doing what 6- and 7-year-old boys do. We were having a pissing contest. We were seeing how high we could pee, with the top of the porcelain being a minimum.

Someone snitched, or a teacher came in at the wrong time, but we were caught and hauled off to the headmistress's office. Miss Bennett was of a certain age at the time and, to us, quite scary.

In the mid-1960s, we risked some form of corporal punishment for our transgressions in many schools, but luckily ours was a little more enlightened, and she gave us lines to write, "I will not do it again", Bart Simpson style.

The others polished them off and were on their way in no time. But not me. Oh no, sir, I would not admit to being wrong, even though I obviously was. Like a dog that looks away when you're talking as if he thinks you can't see him, all I could muster in my lines was, "I didn't do it."

And I sat there. I don't know how long I spent working myself into a state and giving myself a headache. Eventually, Miss Bennett let me go out of compassion because sorry really does seem to be the hardest word.

In her 2010 TED talk, *On Being Wrong*, Kathryn Shultz calls our need to be right, "error blindness" She compares the moment when we suddenly know we're wrong to when Wile E. Coyote follows Roadrunner off the cliff and realises that, unlike Roadrunner, he can't fly. "Most of the time, we don't have any kind of internal cue to let us know that we're wrong about something until it's too late." Gulp. He crashes to the ground.

"But there's a second reason we get stuck inside this feeling —and this one is cultural. Think back for a moment to elementary school. You're sitting there in class, and your teacher is handing back quiz papers, and one of them looks like this. This is not mine, by the way. So there you are in grade school, and you know exactly what to think about the kid who got this paper. It's the dumb kid, the troublemaker, the one who never does his homework. So by the time you are nine years old, you've already learned, first of all, that people who get stuff wrong are lazy, irresponsible dimwits—and second of all, that the way to succeed in life is never to make any mistakes."

Western culture is terrified of "wrong" and making the wrong choice that may or may not have bad consequences. We're good at learning those lessons. I'm also from a generation of kids who could never put their hands up in class for fear of ridicule for getting the answer wrong.

We live in a culture where it's bad to make mistakes. School (and sometimes parents) punish us for getting bad grades, and we'll do anything to stop looking stupid to classmates or colleagues. This all can lead us to being perfectionists. And there is no world where that is good.

There are also dangers in thinking we are right. Katherine Shultz talks about a patient who woke up after an operation with bandages on the wrong leg. The surgeon was so confident he didn't bother to check the details of the procedure.

We are not always right, especially when we are spectacularly wrong. Overconfidence leads to us getting worked up by people disagreeing with us. I can't help feeling that if there was a little more humility in today's world, we might be in a better place.

Being wrong is part of the human condition. It's not always pleasant to realise it, but there's no getting away from it. Twelve hundred years before René Descartes wrote "*Je pense, donc je suis,* St. Augustine wrote "*fallor ergo sum*"—I err, therefore I am." And there's always Wile E. Coyote to give us a laugh. That's not a bad model to follow.

To have to make choices

When you're in a J.O.B., you're protected mainly by the organisation that employs you. You make decisions within guidelines so that you and their arses are covered. If you contrive to make a spectacularly wrong one, you get fired. After that, for most people, there'll always be another job.

On the other hand, business owners make decisions all the time, and there's no one to cover for them. They have to live and die by the choices they make. We can't always see those situations coming. We get blindsided by the bumps in the road. How could we be otherwise? We only foresee a smooth trajectory along a road paved with happiness and gold (sic). When things go wrong, there's no get-out-of-jail-free card, we're on the spot, and we have to deal with the situation. There's no option to get another job.

Which begs the question, how do we deal with bumps in the road in our storytelling? What happens when we realise we made the wrong choice, all in good faith? What happens when we realise we've cocked up?

People like us are fallible humans. That involves being honest with the world and, most importantly, ourselves. Part of my experience was when I realised it was okay to be wrong and not live up to the expectations I had of myself.

We compare our insides to other people's outsides, but we do not know what's happening inside their heads. It's reassuring to know sometimes that other people's insides are often as confused as ours.

I met Shaine Amour a couple of years ago. She's a medium and does a lot of work with energy and spirituality. I'm not sure why because we come from entirely different sides of the beliefs spectrum, but we hit it off. Our transatlantic conversations went on for hours. Even if I don't agree with most of what she believes—and she knows this—we've had some extremely valuable conversations about the energy we carry around and what that means for us as humans.

Her story is also in juxtaposition with the marketing mantras where we're supposed to be on a constant growth trajectory. Growth is the only answer; otherwise, you're a loser. Yet, some people don't want a constantly bigger business; they want one that is smaller but is in line with their values. We're not supposed to want to be small.

Shaine went through a traumatic divorce, and within one year, she lost the grandparents who helped raise her, the father with whom she'd only just been reunited, and then her two kids left due to a custody battle. She hit rock bottom after that flurry of losses. She says her fiancé saw her come home from work and knew something was wrong. He told her she was dying from the inside out. She knew something had to change.

"So, simultaneously around this time is when I received that message from spirit that it's not time to lay down and die. Now it's time to fly. I put it all together. And I chose to get up and focus on helping others to be strong for my kids and me"

She was still working in a comfortable job in the local school district with good benefits as a teaching assistant. However, she knew it was time to move on. She needed to cut the cord with the school district as she'd outgrown it. She was going to be a medium full-time.

She hit the ground running by doing some sessions from home, but she wanted to get out into the public. She landed some gigs in a local metaphysical shop doing readings and grew some good relationships.

Yet the metaphysical shop helped her determine as much what she didn't want as what she did. Too many mediums get caught up in the paraphernalia of being a medium and the seriousness of life. For a spiritualist, she's very much down to earth. She can't work with what she calls the "unnecessary hogwash" of much in the spiritual world. Crystals, burning oil and incense are cinema and show and don't add anything to the experience. Her approach is psychological, helping people reconnect with themselves through their loved ones as a way of getting through the trauma of grief, much like a lot of other counsellors.

She decided the way to get the most from her business was to go back to working from home. Then COVID hit, which forced her to start consulting online.

Her problem was that she started attracting many people who were different from the type of clients with whom she wanted to work. They didn't align with what she was trying to do. So later in the year, she signed up for a major business development program in an attempt to seek out those better suited to what she had to offer.

She wanted to upgrade the environment in which she was working and the type of people she was working with. She was attracting the wrong kind of clients and saw the program as a way of mixing with ambitious people and having some of it rub off on her.

She invested $20,000 in a business development program that would give her a new platform, website and packages to take on the world. She developed three tiers of programs based on weekly calls looking at people's spiritual connections, developing their relationship with "spirit", and bringing them back to themselves, not just making a connection with a loved one. It is a way of developing a relationship with a higher power, but she has a more down to Earth view than many in that world. For her, the stars don't need to be "aligned", and there doesn't need to be a full moon for work to be successful. She says she puts on a show but takes out the unnecessary drama.

Her business does not just involve personal development for the people she works with, but also for herself. She gets all her energy from those one-on-one sessions and the moment of enlightenment when her client suddenly makes the breakthrough and realises their potential or that they've made the connection they're looking for.

Yet, the longer programs with greater commitments didn't seem to work as well despite the work being much more profound. The original spark was missing. Shaine had a dilemma. With effort, she could have built a much bigger business than now if she'd continued with her three-tier conventional product offering setup. She had all the marketing tools at her disposal through the program she'd invested in, and she had the support system. But something needed to align with the basic principles and values she espoused when she started.

After much agonising, she chose to go with her heart and remove the top tier six-month program she was selling for $5,000 and mothball the second three-month one. It's still there if people want it, but they have to show commitment to it, and they're able to invest in it fully. Most of her clients are vulnerable and grieving, and she's very conscious that she shouldn't be exploiting them.

She doesn't think she wasted the $20,000, telling me she had to go through the process to discover her zone of genius and what gives her the most joy. She takes people on a journey that helps them realise who they are and allows them to carry on with their lives after a period of difficulty. Who am I to argue with that?

Business owners always have to make choices. There are always questions about marketing or sales, who to hire, who to let go of, goals and targets. But it's the ones about where their business is going and what it should be doing that are the most difficult.

Or to keep your options open, you never know when you'll need those old skills

Sarah Silva didn't learn any languages in primary school, but she caught the bug very early. Even before she got to secondary school, she made her cousin teach her every French number up to 100. It was the start of a love affair.

But as much as she loved them, she never saw them as a

career. Despite doing French and German at school, no one ever said, "you could be a translator", or suggested any practical use for learning languages. That shows how British schools have always valued foreign languages in schools.

Sarah grew up to be practical. Her father's death when she was just five years old significantly affected her home life as her mother took on the role of both parents. When a builder botched a home extension project that would have given her and her brother separate bedrooms and subsequently disappeared without a trace, the family had to think on its feet.

Her mother raised Sarah and her brother to be self-sufficient. As a result, she had to gain all the skills she could ever need, and all bases had to be covered. They lived in constant disarray for the next seven or eight years, having to do the building work themselves and bringing in contractors whenever the money was available. She learned how to wire a plug and fit a roof tile. Yes, not a typo, a roof tile when she was 15. I've seen the picture. She still does the DIY in the house, although a little less willingly.

Sarah's practical side led her to chemistry, which had more obvious career implications. She was good at it and enjoyed it, but at the same time, she didn't want to ditch the German. I guess that's what you call keeping her and her options as open as possible. Choosing Chemistry and German also meant she could travel, spend some time in Germany, and keep one foot in science and the other in the arts.

She went to Germany "blissfully ignorant of what I was going to encounter", was it an adventure? She was right; it's what you do when you're young. She knew she'd have to improve her everyday vocabulary. She hadn't calculated, however, for Bavarian. Bavarian is either a German dialect or a language in its own right, depending on who you ask. But when you're just getting your bearings in one language, it's damned confusing.

Arriving on a public holiday when everything was shut didn't help. And shut in Bavaria means shut. In the UK, there's always an exception to the rule, always a corner store to get some milk. Not in Bavaria. So she had to go to a youth hostel as the student halls office wasn't open.

The culture shock came with the highly-organised rota for the student halls where she found herself and its seven different types of bin. That wasn't student life as she knew it. And everyone spoke Bavarian. By the end of the year, she'd learned enough to understand and reply, but the road was long and full of incomprehension. She got a job as a waitress at the end just as a way of staying longer.

The immersion was complete and it's the only guaranteed way to learn a language properly. It was so complete that she had trouble getting her words out trying to buy a ticket for the last leg of the journey home at the station in London.

She got a job in a paper mill when she got back "doing chemical trials on buckets of pulp" and managed to pick up some Polish along the way. But no German. It seemed like those two would never get an opportunity to hook up together.

Something still convinced her she couldn't do anything with her growing array of languages because the money was in chemistry. A professor in Germany even told her she was crazy to think she could do anything with Chemistry and German together. Maybe she was spreading herself too thin?

She took time out to travel to Japan, Australia and New Zealand and then South Africa. She landed a job as an English as a Foreign Language teacher when she returned. It was enough to convince her she didn't want to be a teacher—not in a classroom, anyway. But that idea of working with languages just wouldn't go away.

She worked for a flooring manufacturer with mainly German-speaking customers in a multilingual and multinational workplace. She even learned some Spanish, at least enough to get through on the phone to someone who spoke one of her languages better. She had a similar position in a pharmaceutical company, thinking she could use chemistry more.

Well, almost, but not quite. She was still hedging her bets. She got to travel, and the company paid for her to learn Polish. But the opportunities to use her chemistry were limited unless she wanted to be a salesperson in Germany.

After four years, she rediscovered the idea that may have been staring her in the face all along—translation. She didn't want to be a generalist translator as generalists are two a penny. The way forward was as a specialist German to English chemistry one.

The transition was speeded by having met her husband. He had a night job and she had a day job, so they only saw each other as half—asleep ships in the night. Freelance life was attractive because she wanted the flexibility to see her husband, but she was also tired of implementing other people's decisions. She wanted more control over her life, not necessarily to build an empire. Not then, anyway.

It didn't even occur to her that she was giving up the benefits of an employer, like paid leave. The prize was flexibility, and she would make it work. Still covering all bases, she planned out her business in detail before taking the leap. When she handed her notice in, she was prepared to walk away but offered to go part-time for a few months so she could train her successor.

It's only now she realises how valuable that was and how smooth the transition was. She was so over-prepared that when she went to the bank to open a business account, she went with a business plan even though she was not asking for finance. She just wanted an account, not a loan. Her chemistry skills made her quite unusual as a translator, so she got work quickly and replaced her salary within two months. The mix that people found strange earlier was finally starting to pay. I remember being told when I first started translating that there were two types of translator, the specialist and the hungry. It's only now she realises how important that is.

Self-employment brought the freedoms required. Now it was just a question of finding the clients prepared to pay her rates. The business went well enough for her to be able to get married and go on a honeymoon in the first year, take six months maternity leave in the second year and nine months later and build relationships with clients good enough for them to have work for her when she came back. When she returned to work the second time, clients called within hours. That's the power of being a specialist because there was no one around to replace her.

Juggling time with the job and time with the family was starting to become a struggle, and she realised that things would have to change. She had a couple of non-agency direct clients and wanted more. When she started reading books like Tim Ferris' *4-Hour Work Week*, she realised she was more a business owner than a freelancer.

Many translators are notoriously bad at marketing themselves in their box rooms with their academic mindset. Some think marketing is below them, work will just come to them. Increasingly, that is no longer the case.

She was in the process of striking out. She joined Vicky

Quinn Fraser's then Business for Superheroes group to up her game and discovered direct response marketing as a way to engage with potential clients that stands out because so few people are doing it these days. She identified where her weaknesses were and tried to get training in marketing and sales as a way of getting direct clients. That type of training did not exist within the translation industry.

The Superheroes group was pivotal as it was a community of many different professions—engineers, charity workers, ice sculptors, and copywriters (including this one) which broadened her horizons and gave her the sales and marketing training she needed.

It inspired her to write a book about the language perils of international business, which she used as a springboard for a marketing campaign that has allowed her to transition almost exclusively to direct clients and be extremely picky about the agencies she works with. She's started mentoring other translators looking to go down the same path as her. A second book is in the pipeline to show translators that there's a way to beat the boom and bust spending hours in a box room and going nowhere. She's transitioned from a freelancer to a *bona fide* business owner.

We've had many discussions about how she should identify herself. Just a translator? A trainer? A coach? Or a combination of all three. Even though she's not comfortable with the word "coach", she probably is one.

One of the most important things about telling our story is how we identify ourselves. She thinks she might be a trainer, but that doesn't describe the extent of what she does. She's moving into her new role, but slowly. She needs to be prepared. In her final year of primary school, Sarah's teacher said she had the potential to lead but just won't. She thinks she's still very much like that. Although she knows more than enough, she still thinks she doesn't. She even knows how to fit a roof tile.

Expect to be resilient

On her (rather excellent) podcast, The Solo Collective, Rebecca Seal discusses the trials and tribulations—and the good things—about working alone. In her discussion about resilience, Bruce Daisley, author of *The Joy of Work* and champion of making workplaces better places to work, makes some interesting points.

"... I found myself very close to the epicentre of the biggest explosion in peacetime. I was in Beirut last summer when there was this colossal blast in the middle of Beirut last year. And the really interesting thing at the time is that both the New York Times and The BBC said almost identical sentences. "Well if there's one thing we know about the Lebanese people, we know they're resilient people."

The largest peacetime explosion happened in the summer of 2021 in Beirut when 2,750 tonnes of ammonium nitrate exploded, killing 217 people and injuring more than 7,000. At the same time, there was a report in a Turkish newspaper about survivors saying, "fuck resilience; we just want to live our lives."

We fetishise resilience; it's what we expect of "victims" in quite a patronising manner. There's a growing movement of companies with toxic working cultures blaming staff for not being "resilient" enough. "Resilience training", where victims are blamed for not being strong enough, is evidence of gaslighting becoming an Olympic sport.

Simone Biles, probably the greatest gymnast of all time, survived parental abandonment and a drug-addicted mother who ended up going to jail. After a year in care, her grandparents adopted her. She was also a victim of the sexual abuse scandal at the centre of USA gymnastics. She was the poster child for resilience. And yet, when things went wrong in the 2021 Tokyo Olympics, and she couldn't face competition, armchair commentators like Piers Morgan decided she should be more resilient.

As I write this, I feel in a funk. My wife has COVID and is feeling rough. My building site house has seen no developments for a week, and a marketing campaign I'm running is going nowhere. I can't say I'm at my happiest. Some of my old "you're not worthy" demons are rearing their heads again. That is my everyday life, and I know it will pass. It is more resistance than resilience. It's an occupational hazard.

Actual resilience for most business owners should neither be celebrated nor decried. It's described as our ability to bounce back from adverse events and circumstances and has little to do with the proverbial stiff upper lip. It can also be at the heart of our origin stories—some businesses started in extreme adversity.

After almost dying twice before she was 19, Claire Russell set up and sold insurance businesses for nearly 20 years. She cut her teeth, setting up the first brokerage in a Portakabin in Accrington, where she was born. It began with a firm idea of the specialist business she wanted, but she started taking on work that moved it further and further away from her ideals— the specialist she'd wanted to become more and more generalist and eventually lost its sense of purpose. So after four years, she sold it and started again, this time determined to keep it on track and make it successful.

Initially, she had no intention of selling a second time and said so in no uncertain terms when approached out of the blue ten years later by one of the most successful brokerages in the country who wanted to buy it from her and take her on as Operations Director. But the charm offensive worked in the end, and she became an employee for the first time. She told me that her time there was both the best and worst of times. She became responsible for a nationwide network of offices from Padstow to Glasgow, a £350 million budget, all the branch managers and what they did with it. It was thrilling and stressful in equal measure. She learned a tremendous amount, but having young children meant she knew it couldn't last.

She left three years later after being headhunted to be managing director of a large brokerage in Birmingham. The package and the promises made were eye-watering. She was promised autonomy and had a brief to treble the business in the coming years. However, it didn't work out like that. The promises of autonomy were worthless, and every decision she tried to make was blocked. She felt trapped.

Claire's background means she has a well-developed sense of self-worth. She didn't take well to being treated like a child and not trusted to do what she'd been hired to do. She developed acute anxiety and depression, and her drinking escalated out of control. One day on her way to work, she saw a train coming into the station and thought, albeit fleetingly, that if she stepped out in front of it, she wouldn't have to feel like "this" anymore.

That was enough. Claire called the friend who had headhunted her—they'd known each other for ten years—and said she couldn't do it anymore. A doctor signed her off, and she never went back.

She took a year off to decompress and train as a Samaritans volunteer whilst thinking about what to do next. She thought she'd leave the industry after her experience, but an old friend persuaded her to return and do part-time consultancy work.

She was running a network marketing business with characteristic gusto and had met a new partner in 2016 after her marriage broke down. She was happy again. But the realities of life and business are never far apart; sometimes tragedy is a driver towards greater things.

Her partner Mark was trying to rebuild a new life after a crushing personal and professional disappointment. He'd tried many things: network marketing and expensive personal development programs. Nothing seemed to be working. The more he did, the more inadequate he felt. Claire says all those who dangled the carrot of salvation in front of him took advantage of him. Ultimately, it was all too much, and in March 2017, Mark took his own life.

It's an understatement to say Claire was devastated. But a few weeks later, when she was on the floor sobbing her heart out, she heard Mark's voice say to her, "remember who you are." She knew then it was either going to make or break her. Claire isn't one to turn down a challenge.

By May, she knew what she wanted to do and was making plans with a Mental Health First Aid qualification. She was going to start a business providing mental health training and helping managers and staff avoid burnout through her lived experience. We had lunch in a pub in Leamington Spa around that time and I remember being struck by the clarity of purpose and her vision.

As difficult as it was, she was not going to be beaten down by the things in her life. She had a mission to talk about difficult things. There has been a movement towards discussing difficult mental health issues in businesses, but there is a way to go yet. If you sweep the difficult things under the carpet, no one gets to learn about them and they will only repeat themselves again and again.

Business owners always face problems; it's in the job description. They need to get more clients, generate leads, build an email list, and solve everyday problems that are not unlike the things they'd face drawing a salary. But the real stories are those that fall between those cracks. The stories of the unexpected and vulnerability, when we admit to being wrong and grow when life dumps stuff on us. What you do next counts the most. These are the things that make us and don't break us. These are our stories.

Sheena Whyatt didn't either. She'd joined in the Royal Air Force after leaving school, but had to leave when she broke her back in a training incident. She then worked in learning and development for a large American pharmaceutical company. She was particularly unhappy in her job as a trainer when she saw her helicopter pilot husband fly off to the Iraq War in September 2001. As she watched him disappear over the horizon as part of a long line of military wives at 5 o'clock one morning, she didn't know whether she'd ever see him again.

She took the day off, and after talking to a friend that lunchtime and a good amount of Prosecco, she quit her job. She called her boss to say she wasn't going back, and that was that. It was another of those moments where Wile E. Coyote was peddling off a cliff and suddenly realised there was nothing but emptiness beneath him. It may have been the Prosecco talking, but she had no plan. She did see her husband again, and they've been married for 30 years now.

In the meantime, she's run two successful training businesses. After she extricated herself from the first one when her relationship with her business partner turned sour, she was determined the second one was going to be run on her terms. She didn't want to lose control again and was determined to run an organisation she could be proud of. She wanted it to be ethical, where she could care for her trainers properly and not treat them like performing monkeys. It took some time to gain momentum because there were restrictions resulting from the legal battles she was having with her previous business partner, but after a year, things started to pick up.

But 2010 was not a good year for Sheena. Her father died in February, and she was diagnosed with breast cancer in August. She says that people who didn't know her very well expected her to throw in the towel, close her business, and be a "cancer patient" for the next nine months. But Sheena is not like that, far from it. She felt somewhat aggrieved that she wasn't even 40, but she certainly wasn't going to give up. "Cancer is a bastard," she says. So she threw herself at it with gusto. So much so that she arrived at a networking meeting one morning with no memory of how she got there. She was running on empty. That's when she realised she had to slow down a little bit and give herself the best opportunity of recovering.

The next year she'd been shortlisted for a prize with the Learning and Performance Institute. She decided to go to the dinner in the Dorchester in London because it was the night before her penultimate chemotherapy treatment and she knew she would feel as good as she was going to feel. She was at her table talking with people when someone prodded her on her surgical side, asking whether it was her on the big screen in front of them. It was an old photograph, but it certainly was her. She'd won the prize. Walking through the ballroom, she noticed a bit of a disturbance. She thought there was somebody behind her trying to get past, so she stopped and looked behind. But she was, in fact, hearing people getting up and giving her a standing ovation as she walked through the room.

"And when I walked past a table, it had some of the clients I was working with at the time and you know, big guys, Sainsbury's, WH Smith, etc., and somebody said, 'do you know, who's who is this coming by?' And the words I heard were "that's Sheena Whyatt from Lightning Training. And if you want to know what true grit and determination looks like she's walking right past you."

Another lightbulb went off because those were exactly the kind of words she wanted people to say about her. It started a thought process that triggered another change about two years later. She was at a networking meeting talking to our mutual friend Stef Thomas. In her words, "I was having the mother of all whinges." When she let him get a word in edgeways, he asked her what people asked her about when she talked to them. She thought a little and said, "they ask me how I do this, how I'm Sheena Whyatt, how do I do all this stuff?" He looked at her and said, "So why aren't you telling them?"

Boom. The moment of clarity. She realised it wasn't that clients weren't coming to her, it was that she no longer loved what she did. "Nobody was buying because I wasn't buying". She realised she wanted to help people understand how to build a business and how to build a brand. And she's done exactly that. She wants her clients to have a Dorchester moment when they hear what people say about them when they're not in the room.

"I want them to get to the end of that quote that says your personal brand isn't about what people say about you when you're in the room. I want them to add the bit on at the end. 'You have the power to control that dialogue'. You can, Yeah, but those words are out there. It was a lightbulb moment."

Two women and two different experiences of having to face life-changing problems outside their business. Neither of them are victims and don't consider themselves as heroes.

They've dealt with the cards they've been given. Others have faced other tragedies and have not made it through. That doesn't matter because we're not creating league tables of resilience. One person's resilience is no more worthy than the next person's. Bad things get in the way sometimes. Full disclosure, both Claire and Sheena are friends, and I admire them enormously, not because of what they've been through or even because they've come out the other end, but because they are good human beings.

Chapter 8

The Quest For Meaningful Work And What Really Matters

The quest for meaningful work

I was still saying I didn't know what I wanted to do when I grew up well into my fifties. I wanted to be a train driver when I was nine, that didn't work out. Then I wanted to be an architect, that fell on uninformed opinion of a chemistry teacher (not even my chemistry teacher) in a white coat. I wanted to be an academic when I was 21, but I screwed that up all by myself, flunking the final exam and fleeing to France. I didn't have the self-belief to chase that dream anyway.

So I drifted from job to job with no real purpose. I knew in my heart of hearts that I was an intellectual and wanted to be a writer, but I didn't know how to do it and didn't dare to try. I was making it up as I went along, and I certainly wasn't happy.

According to research by Gallup in 160 countries, a massive 85% of the world's full-time workers are unhappy with their work. Blue-collar workers are the most unhappy wherever they are across a wide range of sectors. The higher you go up the management chain, the happier people tend to be. Probably because the higher up you go, the more agency you have.

The picture for the self-employed is a little more nuanced. The Gallup study found that the self-employed are less happy than their employed colleagues. That's a likely reflection of the fact that self-employed life can often be depressing and lonely as we lack the support systems that an employed situation tends to provide. The anecdote is a clear awareness of why we do what we do.

I realised only recently that a sense of purpose in business is central, like a purpose in life. You have to know where you're going. Why did you start? What's the journey, and where are you going? You can find your work meaningful or meaningless. You can have a purpose or not—there's no obligation to do either. But to tell a convincing story, your heart has to be in it.

Human beings are hard-wired to find meaning in everything; as our old friend René Descartes said, "*Je pense, donc je suis*", "I think; therefore, I am." From early human beings onwards, we have always sought to create structure around our lives. As we developed beyond the early hunter-gatherer societies into towns and cities, we created structures and systems that enabled us to grow. Central to that growth was a feeling of common cause centred around religious identity, a notion of territory or one of a clan.

Rightly or wrongly, that sense of purpose and duty in the modern world often centres around work and work culture. We get up; we go to work and do meaningful things. Then we come home and relax with things that have less meaning. That has been the cycle since the nineteenth century. But work is changing and many of us no longer see the 9-to-5 as the goal. Technology is making flexible working easier as we demand more from our lives.

If you base your perception of business owners on The Apprentice/Shark Tank and programmes like that, you might take a dim view of them as a tribe. And you'd be right; there are a lot of scumbags around. They're the people who give the rest of us a bad name, those who are there to take what they can and to hell with the consequences. They're the ones with the ridiculous power poses, shoulder pads and red braces.

Fortunately, most businesses don't work like that. They are in the game of earning an honest living and trying to make the world a better place. I wrote this book, in part, for them. I wanted to get those businesses to tell their stories and talk about the simple things, why they started and the problems they faced along the way.

But what keeps them going? What drives them? What is their role and where do they find meaning?

In her rather excellent book, *Solo*, an exploration of working alone, Rebecca Seal asks, "What is meaningful work?" If you pinned her down to one job, she'd say she's a journalist. She spent many years working for newspapers like The Guardian and The Observer and working in restaurants. She's now a freelance writer with several recipe books to her name, is a newspaper contributor and has presented on TV. More recently, she's fronted a podcast about working solo based on her book.

Rebecca grew up surrounded by people who did "meaningful" work, and it seemed logical that she would follow in their footsteps. Her parents were both social workers, so she's always thought public service and meaningful work went together. When she was 15, she decided—as only 15-year-olds can—she would work for the United Nations, the biggest and boldest version of public service there is.

Unfortunately, Rebecca's post-graduate degree failed to

woo the United Nations or any of the other international organisations to whom she applied. She'd wanted to follow in her parent's footsteps and did a Master's degree in International Relations. She'd planned to work for a non-governmental organisation in conflict alleviation or mine clearance. But it was while researching her thesis on conflict resolution and genocide she realised that kind of work wasn't for her. She couldn't expose herself to that level of horror regularly without it having a massive psychological impact. She also knew she couldn't be a nurse, a midwife, or any other jobs people say are "caring." But that didn't mean she didn't look for meaning and purpose in her work. She'd gone into adulthood with the express intention of making some impact on the world.

She worked for several years in the hospitality industry, but it didn't feel like it had status compared to the work of her parents, social workers, or friends. She says she was an "okay" restaurant manager, but not a great one.

"I am not good at repeated, let's say, intimate interactions with members of the public. I'm not good at tolerating people's predilections for a particular heat level in their coffee. I am not good at dealing with people on a Friday night over and over and over again, I worked in restaurants for seven years. I'm really good at serving food and remembering orders. I'm good at thinking about menus and the spaces in which people might want to be entertained—I can do all that. I don't like people grabbing me because they want an order to be taken. I have a low tolerance for the degree of impoliteness you experience when you're in the service industry in the UK."

"So for me, it's about figuring out not just the things that you enjoy, but how you thrive and then allowing yourself to accept that it can be meaningful. But it absolutely has status as meaningful because it meant something to me. And it brought, you know, joy and entertainment to other people."

We can't all be doctors, nurses, and all-round saints. Rebecca has found her sense of purpose in her writing about, as her website says, "the things which make us human: work, family, food, drink and health." And who doesn't get pleasure from a recipe book?

Writing this book has been a journey of discovery for me. It started with me realising I had something worth saying. It concludes with the idea that we all have something worth saying and our audience is much bigger than we think.

Like Rebecca and all the other people I've spoken to, we all do what we do in some measure to make the world a better place. The link between meaning and story is close. If you want to engage with an audience truly, finding meaning in what you do that goes beyond making money will give them a reason. Otherwise, you risk having a purely transactional relationship, where fidelity is never a priority.

Vicky and the quest for a meaningful path

Sometimes, the world just punches you in the gut and says, "Now hang on, let's just throw everything you believed previously up in the air and start again." The events of 2020 changed things forever for many business owners. We faced things we'd never encountered before. They made many of us reassess our values and what we wanted from life.

The search for meaning was already quite the Yellow Brick Road. The lucky ones, the Kira Hugs or Joanna Wiebes have always been clear on their direction of travel, if not the stopovers along the way. The rest of us have had to walk a sometimes tortuous path that is never linear. They are Michelle

Dallys and me, who had no idea they would end up running their own business.

Vicky Quinn Fraser also came to her interpretation of meaning via a sometimes tortuous succession of trial and error. She's far from the only one to say her definition of success is far different now from what it was pre-2020. That was a year that changed priorities for many of us.

She feels she's partly successful already as she makes a good living and has a nice lifestyle renovating an 18th-century cottage. However, her goal for the future is to provide a vehicle for traditionally suppressed voices. She wants to run a publishing house for women authors, people of colour, people with disabilities or LGBTQ+ writers and give them another platform in the growing movement outside the traditional network of publishing houses.

Like so many of us, the world of employment never managed to pin her down to one career; she couldn't follow a traditional path. She did temporary jobs for a while before university but finished the work in half the allotted time, so she'd fill her hours learning to touch type—a skill to be used to great effect later on—and expand her mind by reading or writing.

She loved studying archaeology and ancient history at university as a mature student. That led to a succession of research and investigation posts, some of which she loved more than others. She thought leaving a job she loved so she could be closer to home would be a sound move. It wasn't. She'd walked to the job from hell with a perfect storm of a bad employer and a toxic workplace combined with deteriorating mental health. It caused her to slam the door in the classic "you can't sack me cos I quit" scenario. Like so many of us, employee is not Vicky's role in life.

She got a lifeline with freelance copywriting from a friend who ran a design agency she'd introduced to her employer to get her started in a business. She'd always wanted to run her own business, and suddenly, necessity and opportunity combined to push her into taking the leap. She'd already made plans as a 16-year-old, filling notebooks with ideas for the business she was going to run and had even started prospecting for clients for Sunflower Secretarial Services. But at that age, "that's not what you do: you go to school and college, you get married and have children." That was the end of that, and she did what she was told. Now, it was real.

She struggled with the poverty pay you find on job boards working ridiculous hours just to pay the bills, but with time, she got good at copywriting and built up a good portfolio of clients. She could have carried on like that and been very successful, but somehow, she never cared enough to become great at it. She says she always preferred content writing, so when someone asked her to help write a book in 2014, she took the opportunity despite not knowing how to do it. After all, what could possibly go wrong? Business life is often about taking opportunities when they present themselves and not waiting to be ready. She took a leap of faith and jumped.

It's taken time, but she's finally managed to carve out the type of business she's happy with. She would have done it earlier if it weren't for societal pressure to be "normal." She just felt "weird" (her word, not mine) in "normal" situations and learned early on not to behave in ways that people think are "too much."

She says she's been "Happily married with self-doubt for 42 years." In many people, that would be crippling—me included—but not for people like Vicky. Her mentor early on, Peter Thomson, said, "when she decides to do something, she does it." Like Amy Harrison, she's not going to let the bullshit stop her from having fun. Once they decide, they take action. Neither of them will let their or anyone else's doubts get in the way of what they want to do.

One of the most precious things about self-employment is if we have the balls, we have complete control over what happens when we get up in the morning. We can control the narrative of our lives by not being dependent on what other people think or do. When Vicky wrote her first book in her name as a copywriter in 2015, it greatly impacted her confidence level. She knew then she was capable of doing "the big stuff."

The second book, "How The Hell Do You Write A Book", changed her beyond recognition and put her in charge of her narrative. The turning point was dropping the idea of "this is how you should behave" or "this is who you should be." No one is or should ever entirely be themselves in their marketing. We always keep a little behind, if nothing else, for our sanity. Now she feels free enough to be who the hell she wants to be. You don't need to be a hustling Gary V or a perma-smile Marie Forleo or Amy Porterfield to get on; you don't need a "magic formula", and trying to be someone else is exhausting. Seth Godin says, "find your weird." That doesn't necessarily mean being goofy; it means finding yourself and assuming that self. And finding people to walk with you on that journey. They are there.

Vicky has completed her transition to full-time book coach, and, to be honest, you wouldn't be reading this book if it wasn't for her. She's found her purpose in making minor differences in people's lives. She says we get afraid to go back in time because we think the smallest thing could change the course of history, but we won't make a small change in the present to change the future because we think there is no point.

All these stories matter because those changes are important. We can spend our lives going through the motions to make someone else rich—our joys and purposes may well lie elsewhere. But when we work for ourselves, we make little differences, sometimes, one person at a time. When Vicky was having a difficult time as a copywriter, wondering if it was what she really wanted to do for the rest of her life, she realised it was a step on a journey. "I can change this to make it less sucky." March 2020 was the opportunity to make that change. "If I'm going to make this work, I need to put the effort in to get better. I need help to do it." And it worked.

That is what this book is all about. I wanted to talk about everyday stories that never see the light of day. They are stories of people you never heard of, but they are yours and mine too. We can find meaning in what we do; the challenge is getting it out.

Amanda couldn't take it anymore

She was a cop in a 520-square-mile patch in rural Ohio fighting a losing battle. She had the late shift - 4 till midnight - when all the bad things happened, responding to all the domestic violence calls, burglaries, and street fights. What's more, and don't believe what you see on TV, she had no partner. She was in the car on her own. That's enough to stress anyone out.

Being a police officer in the US in the twenty-first century was hard going for someone like Amanda. She's in touch with her inner self and questions how she interacts with the world. She likes to see the best in people. So having to disguise herself when she went out or not using her service car to pop home at lunchtime because she was afraid of being identified was hard on her. It was not why she did her job.

Something was wrong—seriously wrong. She was in danger of losing her soul. And who knows what else? "I'd met my now husband, and we'd been dating for just a few weeks and took a spontaneous trip to Nashville. When we were on our way back, I realised I could no longer keep doing what I was doing.

It hit me like a ton of bricks that I just couldn't go back. I took a colossal risk, and he said he would do everything he could to support me. He wasn't lying. He moved in after just two months of dating.

My savings meant money wasn't a problem. I made the jump. I went to the doctor the next day and talked about treatment for depression and PTSD. I got a work excuse for the following two weeks, and I went in at some point that week and put in my notice. I didn't tell them why; I just said it was personal and thanked the department for everything. It was a slow build-up, but that was the shifting moment, realising after just a couple days of freedom that I needed to back away from law enforcement. I'd started yoga in the police academy and took it up again to relieve the stiffness and the stress when I burned out."

Yoga allowed her to breathe and take stock. After all that intensity, she could finally regain control of life. She felt she could breathe again—for the two months between leaving the police and starting another job, she slept up to 18 hours a day.

So she decided to become a yoga instructor. She wanted to develop her well-being and affect others—particularly her former colleagues. But as a woman who doesn't do things by halves, she did so while working full time and planning a wedding. Oh, she also did a Master's degree for good measure.

She was just repeating the habits of her previous life. Only when she gave up her job could she take a step back and assess things.

Amanda's role in life is to help people. She's seen and felt the dangers of poor mental health and wants to help others avoid them. Her 5-year plan is to have enough funds to start a non-profit to be called Lauren's Legacy Foundation after her best friend growing up who took her own life at age 17 with everything ahead of her. All because she didn't have the tools to cope with being a brilliant teenager, and no structures were available to help her.

Lauren was the kind of person who was good at everything. She was in line to be valedictorian and varsity letters. She was a top performer in sports and the symphonic chorale. She was also a singer, and she'd played the lead in Guys and Dolls in the school play, and she was in the Key Club.

"She was brilliant. And she was fearless. But she couldn't see herself clearly, and because she was so young, she didn't realise that all the pain she was feeling could be eased or was temporary."

She was different, but the National Honor Society didn't accept her as a valedictorian—because she had pink hair and didn't dress like everybody else.

I was surprised when Amanda told me that because attitudes like that wouldn't have shocked me when I was Lauren's age in the 1970s, but they beggar belief in the twenty-first century.

"She was so brilliant", Amanda said, "she was herself, and not everybody accepted that. And I think that was very hard for her. Even though mental health issues ran in her family, I think the bigger picture in what I'm doing is getting people to see themselves clearly." For the sake of Lauren.

Amanda is a qualified life coach and yoga instructor now and has found her purpose. She uses everything she's learned to help former colleagues and first responders across the board respond to the mental health challenges their jobs throw at them.

She remembers the stress of not wanting to be recognised in the street or in a grocery store all too well. She thought, "You need a safe place to learn how to breathe, to learn how to calm your mind, and get a respite from all the chaos." And it's working. She's getting noticed by influencers in her industry and, more important, people of influence in law enforcement. She's found her inner peace and her purpose and knows what it's like for those in the thick of it.

Chapter 9

Getting Ideas Above Your Station And Other Revolutionary Thoughts That Will Set You Free

You can tell your story however you want

As I write this, James Hutchinson has launched his new men's fashion brand online. It's the result of the monumental change in mindset he's been through in the last few years caused by losing a third of his body weight. He told me he didn't think he had anything particularly interesting to say.

Cara Mackay runs a (posh) shed business in central Scotland. She does have things to say and is not afraid to say them. Her LinkedIn bio says, "Work my ass off day in day out, in the vain hope that one day I'll make enough money so my Dad and Uncle Grant can retire and I can finally follow my dreams of world domination." She just proposed to her partner on LinkedIn, telling people not to "AT me about LinkedIn not being Facebook" because her partner isn't on Facebook. And why shouldn't she propose on LinkedIn? She's had more than one run-in with the LinkedIn police, but more of that later.

Ash Ambirge grew a multimillion-dollar copywriting

157

business, saying exactly what she thought of the rest of the world. She then ditched the name, The Middle Finger Project, because it had become a millstone around her neck, and she couldn't do anything new.

Wouldn't you be interested in what they had to say? You'd want them to be authentic and honest, irrespective of how they told their stories.

So why do so many businesses hesitate to share their stories? We learned when we were young that bragging was bad, that no one likes a show-off, and even in the twenty-first century, not to get ideas above our station. But there's more to it than that. People want you to be real.

Customers are increasingly seeing through traditional sales pitches and are looking for other ways to engage with brands. They want connection, meaning and a way to identify with you. Especially—although not exclusively—younger generations are turning away from consuming for consumption's sake. Now they are not looking for relationships over transactions. Most businesses are slow to take up the baton, though. The traditional way of communicating is safe. Anything else means exposing themselves, and many find that scary.

Brands like Apple or Nike inspire almost fanatical loyalty. They've known how to identify with heroes through their campaigns like the 1984 movie ads for the launch of the Mac, the "Here's to the crazy ones" in Apple's Think Different campaigns or Nike's identification with Michael Jordan throughout the 90s and early 2000s. They've identified markets they want to target and excluded the others by putting stories at the centre of their marketing. They've identified the audiences with whom they wanted to build that relationship. Your party has to have an exclusive guest list if you want to build a relationship. You can't invite everyone to your party because it would be a terrible one.

Showing up is central to building a relationship, but there are plenty of ways of doing that. You don't have to do dancing videos on TikTok any more than you have to do "serious", and "professional" posts on LinkedIn. It's entirely up to you. FYI, I don't.

Adopting this or that style of advertising or marketing has little bearing on whether or not you come across as unique. Your story will do that. You may feel uncomfortable telling some of the details—I know I did. There's a difference between being uncomfortable and doing it anyway and shirking responsibility and hiding away. Business people always do things that make them uncomfortable; that's how they grow—it's in the job description.

If you want to be the next Gary Vaynerchuk and be everywhere all the time, go ahead. But we're not all comfortable with that and shouldn't feel guilty because we fail to reach those levels of visibility. I haven't got the energy. Do whatever makes you feel more comfortable. My style is more laid back and much less aggressive, and while I haven't achieved his level of success yet, I'm quite happy being faithful to who I want to be.

Marketing isn't always about shouting from the hilltops, you can also be calm and collected about it. No one likes the sound of their own voice. So much so that the feeling has a name—voice confrontation. We receive the sound of our own voice through the air and through our bones. When we listen back without the benefit of bone conduction, we sound nothing like we think we sound. We sound like others hear us. I remember the first few times I heard my voice playing back on the videos I'd recorded of calls with clients and being horrified.

I got used to it just by listening back to myself constantly. I'm doing the same with video now.

I say this not as an expert but through personal experience; the only way you can get comfortable with doing things you feel uncomfortable doing is by practice. Don't think of it as going out of your comfort zone—that's such a negative expression—but as the trained-to-within-an-inch-of their-lives-to-expect-everything Navy Seals say, think of it as expanding your zone of competence.

You can record little voice notes to yourself or others or shoot quick videos on your phone that no one needs to see until you're comfortable. These are all little practice sessions to get you more at ease with your presence and how others perceive you. We all have to start somewhere. Even the aforementioned Gary V's early wine videos are atrocious by his own admission. If he can get good, we all can. In any way you please.

The opinions of others

I was scrolling through LinkedIn yesterday and came across one of those posts by someone with whom I'm not connected, but it had 20,000 comments, so it must have been important. This person had posted a happy photo of his wedding to the love of his life—who happened to be another man.

Right on cue, tinged with a large dose of homophobia, the "this is not appropriate" LinkedIn police were out in force. The big downside of social media, and LinkedIn in particular is that it is full of judgemental people. People with their opinion of how you should run and market your business. Many will not like it if you show up with your story and a genuine voice and will have plenty to say about it—especially if you drop in a cuss word or two.

Cara Mackay did just that. She runs Gillies and Mackay, a manufacturer of rather gorgeous sheds, garden rooms, summer houses and garages in Perth in Scotland.

She's at odds with what she calls "the corporate world, the leadership industry or the sort of 'professional' elements of what business is." She has no desire to do all the fakery and pomp and ceremony and "people bullshitting through their business experiences" that often happens on LinkedIn.

"I feel that it's just never been something that's attracted me in a sense of how I want to behave. I've got no desire to be like everybody else when it comes to business and I don't compete with anyone, either. So when you see people normally on LinkedIn, they're usually showing off about winning awards, or seeing how amazing they are, and criticising other people's ways of doing things because "it's not the professional way to do it." That sort of conversation doesn't excite me, I'm much, much more interested in the real life aspects of running a business and being honest with yourself when things are hard."

In early 2017, she wrote a post about her life as a business owner and an (at the time single) mother. This is just the beginning:

> "It's 8 am—you've been up since 5 and you're getting the kids ready for school, or at least out the door. He's fannying about still half in his jammies, half in his uniform. You shout for the MILLIONTH time: "Shoes lad, where's your shoes?!"
>
> In among the spilt cat food and three-day-old wet washing you think: 'fuck, I've got that quote to do before 9am, follow up with that customer from yesterday, check the financial reports and get back to that guy who wants me to do some event thing...'
>
> You return from the school run only to find that you've

forgotten it's shitting blue wheelie bin day! Not to mention a lingering doubt about the integrity of your 8-year-old's ability to hand over dinner money. You're resigned to the fact that the drive to the office isn't going to work, you've got too much to do and the afternoon meetings are closer to home. So... what do you do?"

The post was written in the moment, as most of us do, and she never thought anyone would read it. She says thinking that way enables you to be more honest with things. She was just describing a day in her life as a business owner fighting fires. She thought she'd just publish it quickly and get on with her day. She called it *"How To Fucking Work From Home."*

The results were electric. When I last looked, there were 2,135 comments. 80% of them were positive from people who recognised themselves in what she said. "Hilarious but very realistic", "I love this post. A one-woman rallying cry to actually write something real on LinkedIn, in an authentic tone of voice. Brilliant."

The criticism too, was vociferous. Comments like "Could have made the same point without expletives", "Good article tainted by the use of expletives..... No need!", "Is this appropriate language for this professional website?" It generated local coverage in Scotland, and the growth in sales was exponential.

Shortly after, she wrote about people asking for discounts. That one was even more successful and got national press coverage. "I was a business owner telling people not to bother asking for discounts because they're not going to get one. It's like asking me to go down to the workshop and take 10 pounds out of my dad's back pocket. A lot of people shy away from confrontational conversation, especially when it's to do with customers—the customer's always right, and you've got to bend over backwards for the customer and all the rest of it."

"Whereas I take a much more equal tone with my customers, I educate them as well as I possibly can, so they can make the buying decision for themselves. And I'm a massive advocate of that type of selling. I've got no interest in hard sales. And ultimately, if somebody isn't willing to pay for the product as it is, then they're not the right fit for me."

It's refreshing for most because many people struggle with pricing. No, everyone struggles with pricing. It was a refreshing take for people to give them permission to charge their worth and not make apologies for not discounting. Don't assume one person deciding they don't want to pay what you want to charge means you have to concede control over what you're pricing.

The negative comments I got were all from men of a certain age and demographic who have issues with outspoken women —especially young women. There's a lot of anger and resentment to do with how they want other people to behave, and being upset when somebody doesn't conform to that. And just generally just not liking the fact that you can be successful in business, and stay true to the person you are without conforming to the societal rules around what it means to be a "professional."

And it continues, the more I expose myself to that environment, the more I see it clearer, every time of the sort of misconceptions, the way that people behave and treat others for the way that they look, sound or act in terms of whether or not the other the industries as a whole would accept them.

So I still have that view of LinkedIn. And I still post stuff that's relevant to me and what I'm trying to do here and share my experiences for the people who are willing to admit to themselves what actually running a business is like"

There is much on social media and in the wider world of the bucket of crabs whereby if one crab tries to climb out, the others will try to pull it back and make it fall into line even if it means everyone not surviving. If you put your head above the parapet, you're going to upset someone. But that says more about them than it does about you. You make them feel uncomfortable and they feel challenged by your success.

As Cara says, the negative comments largely came from white, middle-aged men (holding my hand up here, but not joining in, they may be my demographic, but they are not my people) who felt challenged by a young, forthright and successful woman. She's grounded and knows where she's going. She also gives as good as she gets in the comments, so that probably confounds the situation.

You have a voice too. You have a way of doing business. You don't need to be like Cara if that doesn't suit you. It's probably not my style either.

You don't need to put on a show, people like imperfect

"Perfectionism is the voice of the oppressor, the enemy of the people. It will keep you cramped and insane your whole life."
Anne Lamott

Take too close a look at Instagram or any other social platform, and you'll see nothing but perfection. Especially from the big hitters, every sector has them. We are creatures of comparison, and it's very hard not to get paralysed by the thought that we'll never be "that" sound, so what's the point?

You can tell your story in any way you like, but it's not always that straightforward. Introverts and shy people across the world will cringe at the idea of dancing on an Instagram Reel or TikTok or sometimes even just posting on LinkedIn. We are not all born with the self-confidence of Cara Mackay, Joanna Wiebe or Fabi Paolini. But you don't need to. Joanna Wiebe has almost no social media presence, and Cara Mackay limits herself to Linkedin and Instagram and won't go anywhere near Twitter. Fabi Paolini is on Facebook daily, sends emails daily, and often goofs around on Instagram and TikTok. All three have entirely different ways of managing their stories and their success.

I've never found self-promotion easy and I still don't. For years, I thought I was an introvert because I was shy, which was why banging my drum didn't come naturally. But I also realise that I love the company of other people. Those big, never-ending Sunday lunches in France where we'd sit around a table into the evening, putting the world to rights? The big face-to-face networking meetings that, to be honest, were more about talking and making friends than doing any real business? The Zoom calls I've had recently with people across the world that can last two hours or more? I guess I'm not as introverted as I thought, a shy extrovert perhaps?

To be quite frank, writing this book is one of the most challenging yet liberating things I've ever undertaken. My friends have encouraged me, and people close to me have said they want to read it. But I have no idea how the outside world will receive it outside. That is scary and exciting at the same time.

We all have a truth to tell, and we don't need to compare

ourselves to anyone, megastars or even just stars. We are enough. Before you accuse me of woo-woo psychobabble, let me qualify. One of the hardest things you will ever do is to admit your vulnerability. But it's also one of the most liberating. You don't need to be perfect; you have it in you. Self-acceptance is the key.

Just ask yourself what would your audience think about you being perfect. Unless they're living a glossy magazine fantasy, no one is interested in perfection; people don't relate to it. The unattainable lives of the super-successful are just that, unattainable. I'm guessing your audience isn't perfect either.

Perfect is also dull. The news cycle is full of things that go wrong, people who make mistakes, and people with flaws and rough edges. These are what attract us because they make us memorable and unique.

Perfect is limiting and rare. It's very difficult to keep up because you may hit the spot occasionally, but you won't make it every time. The world just isn't like that.

Lastly, perfect is an excuse called procrastination. "I will be happy when" is a great reason to do nothing. I know that because I spent years as a world champion at getting ready. Then life throws a curve ball at you.

It took me a long time to write this book. I was waiting for the right time and comparing myself to others a little too much. They all seemed so ahead of me. But I would never have written it had I stayed like that. It will never be perfect, and that's the joy of creative work.

Your audience is looking for someone just like them, perhaps slightly further down the line and with something to teach them.

The most striking thing that Margo Aaron ever said to me was that just because you write the story that must be told, you are under no obligation to publish it. When I started writing in anger a couple of years ago, I wrote 20,000 words in three weeks. Some of it has found its way into this book, but most of it will never see the light of day. It was me emptying my brain. You can try that too, for practice because no one will ever see. I did videos, too—there are some truly terrible videos on my phone where I mumble, stumble and make a fool of myself. But once I'd gotten over that, I was fine. I was happy with myself, and I'd started to develop my style. You can do the same.

Ash Ambirge and the choice between brand and purpose

When you hang your brand identity around a name like The Middle Finger Project, there can be little doubt about what you stand for; you are making a firm statement of intent. In many ways, Ash pointed Middle Finger in question firmly at corporate America and cubicle life. Not for her the picket fences and 2.4 kids that the American Dream promised. Oh no, Ash was like Samantha from Bewitched with a wicked smile, a bit of magic and a refusal to conform. In contrast, poor old useless Darren and Corporate America could only look on hapless and helpless.

It was insanely successful. In the years since Ash started in 2009, it has drawn a massive following and has allowed her to attract large corporate clients and students to her courses. The MFP was a massive "fuck you" to corporate America. It was proof that you could be a digital nomad successfully and not live in places where the cost of living is so low that anyone earning slightly more than survival rates would look like a gazillionaire. It started when she finally decided that corporate life was not for her. She now lives in Costa Rica but has moved all over the US and Europe and had a spell in Chile. As I write this, she is in Mexico City.

You don't know that people notice you until you touch them. I've been on her email list almost since the beginning of her business in 2009 and was one of the early buyers of her first ebook. It turns out she'd clocked me too, and we've had a very long-distance relationship without much communication ever since. Spending three hours on a Zoom call together more than 5,000 miles and a 7-hour time difference apart was like talking to an old mate.

Perhaps with the passing of time, perhaps with increased maturity or just changing priorities, Ash no longer feels the need to be the rebel child railing against corporate America. It was becoming a millstone and she craved something else. Proudly, she says that with a name like that, she's never been able to place a Facebook ad and her growth has been entirely organic. But it required her to be always "on" and people were disappointed if they didn't get the wild, crazy Ash of her public persona. It may be a little secret, but she actually is not like that. She's a normal, thinking—in fact, quite reflective, human being. We had a very long conversation sharing stories. She does have a hearty-sized laugh on her, though.

She realised the extent of the problem when the Middle Finger Project book was published in 2020. She was pulled from the Today Show because a book with that title could never be mentioned on national TV, she couldn't advertise on Amazon because of the name either and Facebook prevented a friend from posting a link to the site because it contained "inappropriate content." The content is sassy but hardly inappropriate.

She's been so proud of her brand in the past, but now she was starting to feel it's time to move on. In 2021, she launched a

90-day email course, Meat and Hair, to help aspiring and not so aspiring writers with their creativity. She was also writing more travel pieces, all of which didn't fit the Middle Finger Project brand. She feels she can no longer use it as a container for all her ideas.

She told me that after posting weekly and sometimes more on it for 13 years, The Middle Finger Project has more than 500 posts on it. That's a lot of content and a lot of eyes on it.

After a lot of agonising, she decided in the summer of 2022 that it had to go. It was time to move on from the brand that had made her name for the previous thirteen years. It had run out of steam and was no longer fit for purpose.

Now she's starting again from scratch. She told me of the thrill of looking at a website with no posts on it. I have no fears about her ability to fit it with content. *Selfish Forever, An Irreverent Guide to Working Anywhere* reflects her as she is now; she'll be writing about travel, culture and living in countries where she was not born. She could have continued the Middle Finger Project, it was very successful, but it got to the point where it was unbearable. There are many reasons why she let it go, but ultimately, she did it because it felt right. Like any difficult decision, we do it because it chimes with our values, our sense of purpose and because it is meaningful. I don't care what anyone says about fake worthiness, virtue signalling or any other pseudo-insults they think they're hurling. I have just one rule for personal conduct. Live within your values and don't be a dick.

Progress is ... kicking yourself up the butt

You have no right to hide your story away. It's yours and the thing that makes you genuine and unique. It's your glory; it's your treasure to delve into to delight and intrigue your audience. I also know more than most that telling your story can be one of the most intimidating things you can do. I spent years and years hiding, comparing myself to others and running away when the opportunity arose to do something I found a little scary. I have a history of not doing things I desperately wanted to do because they scared me.

I remember at some point in the mid-1960s standing on the platform at the still under-reconstruction Euston station by an in-steam Evening Star. The Evening Star was the last ever steam engine made by British Rail, and it now stands in the National Railway Museum in York. Even then, I knew it was a big deal when I was given the opportunity to stand on the footplate. I was terrified and couldn't do it.

In my twenties, I was in a dull, dead-end job I'd have given anything to leave. I met a recruiter who said I'd be a perfect fit as a management consultant. I wanted to give it a go. I thought I'd be good at it. I was too scared to make the phone call to even get the interview. That was the end of that.

I've lost count of the freelancer jobs I've been in the running for but didn't take because I didn't think I was good enough.

I struggled for years with being visible. I'd get a glimpse and hide away. One time, back in the days when I did face-to-face networking, I faked a comfort break when it was almost my turn to stand up and do my presentation. Of course, the fatal flaw in that plan was they offered me the opportunity to do it when I got back into the room. I could hardly say no. I'd been found out.

I spent years feeling I was almost there; greatness was just around the corner. But, it was perpetually just around the corner. We all have reasons not to make the move, not to step into greatness. We're not quite ready, we listen to other people who think it's not a good thing to do, and circumstances are never quite right. Most of the time, it's just us getting in our own way.

Then the events of 2020 changed how I saw the world. Not long before, when I was helping my ailing mother out of my car, I suddenly realised that the roles had reversed. She was no longer the caregiver; I was the adult in the room. When she went to the care home, I was the point of contact, I had the power of attorney along with my wife and brother, and we had to make the critical decisions.

Ultimately, I had to tell a doctor that she should only come out of hospital for palliative care. The five-year-old in me was screaming, but what could he do? I organised the funeral—the second one in less than two years after my uncle had died in 2018—and organised the probate. Just like a grown up.

I'd pulled together some family photos for the wake and saw my life on a screen. There were pictures of me as a child and my mother in her late 20s and others in her mid-80s. That was when it hit me. This was my life, and it was no longer a rehearsal; I was no longer getting ready. My mother was 26 when I was born. That's my yardstick. It was time to face all those fears and that imposter syndrome. It was time to and grab the proverbial bull by the horns.

I picked up on Margo Aaron's writing voice program from one of her emails that had been languishing in my inbox for a couple of months. The sales page had the effect on me that every copywriter dreams of. She joined the conversation I'd been having in my head for years, so I begged her to let me in. I just knew it was what I needed.

When we worked together, I went in prepared to be open and vulnerable with her. After all, what did I have to lose?

What purpose would it have served to hide things from her? I hadn't reckoned on her digging into my shame. All the shame I probably wasn't aware I was feeling over the cavernous gap between my aspirations and the reality of my life.

She encouraged (told) me to do Seth Godin's altMBA. It was full of people who previously I would have thought way beyond my pay grade. It was full of tasks previously I'd have never thought myself capable of doing. It changed my life. I realised I was good enough. I had met my people and my zone of genius.

I'm still a work in progress, we all are. I've joined a mastermind for high-flying copywriters and am looking forward to what that will give me. Because if not now, when? After being aware of it for so many years and thinking it was so far away, I can no longer say, "When I'm Sixty-Four", so I'd better make the most of it.

I think it all starts with owning the situation and self-acceptance. That's the best way of not falling flat on your face or making a fool of yourself. That's how people want you to be, you can't keep up the fakery unless you have superhuman powers of deception. People will see through it, anyway. You don't need to be dancing on Instagram Reels if that makes you uncomfortable. You can turn up in any way that feels right. But turn up you must.

Get rid of ideas you may have about how you're supposed to come across. Just being natural is more comfortable, and it's the best way to persuade your audience to do whatever you want them to do. It's very difficult to avoid going over the top and into full-on woo about this. It really is a question of being genuine and finding your true self. That means forgetting many preconceived ideas about how you should be and shouldn't be and releasing that energy inside you to make you who you always wanted to be.

That can often come through the voices of others. I had a number of "meet and greet" calls in a workshop I did at the beginning of 2022 with conversations with copywriters across the world, from California to New Zealand. I gained from that people were interested in what I had to say. They kept saying how much they loved my stories. So once you see people can accept you for who you are and not who you think they want you to be, it'll be time to get down to work.

There's no simple solution to this. Your subconscious will fight you tooth and nail and put things in the way. "What if I'm not good enough?", "What if people ignore me?", "What if some people hate me?" These are all possibilities.

I'll tell you a secret. I feel quite awkward writing this because I'm experiencing all of those emotions right now. It's called Resistance, and it's there to protect you even if you don't want to be protected. It helps us make up all kinds of reasons not to do what you have to do. Steven Pressfield opens *The War of Art* with the idea that we have two lives, the life we live and the unlived one within us. "Between the two stands Resistance. Resistance is the most toxic force on the planet. It is the root of more unhappiness than poverty, disease, and erectile dysfunction."

Resistance manifests itself best in procrastination. It means that we don't think we'll never do our thing, write that blog post, that email or make that video, just not today. Until the next day comes, the one when we were supposed to take the action, and we have another excuse. And so it goes on. And don't tell me you've never done that because I know you have.

Those shenanigans could go on forever. I made a good attempt, and I had to wait until I was on the wrong side of 60 until I snapped out of it. I started by writing a book and will continue in the future, helping other business owners tell their story.

Taking the first step is daunting. Starting at a blank sheet of paper and not knowing what to say is intimidating, but you've got this. It'll be fine.

Conclusion

F ive years ago, I had no idea I was going to write a book, let alone this one. Even when I was finishing the last passages, I got quite giddy. "A book? Who am I to write a book?" I'd always been a reader; writing, on the other hand, was what authors did. I wasn't an author.

I'd had a few ideas to write a book over the years, but most were terrible. I'd convinced myself I hadn't done anything significant. There are plenty of books on copywriting in circulation; no one wants another. No one would be interested.

When I eventually started at 62, I did what I do best: I talked. I spoke to people I knew from my years of face-to-face networking and gradually beyond that circle of friends. It suddenly dawned that everything I'd been saying about myself was hokum. I only recently realised I have one thing that no one else has. My experience. No one can take that from me. People were interested in what I had to say, and I could help them coax their stories out of them too.

I'd read Bernadette Jiwa's book, Story Driven, and was bitten by a bug. I saw marketing as something to be done with real people who care, their genuine stories at the centre of things.

The stories in this book stand on their own. They don't have any particular importance, but they are all incredibly important at the same time. Some are dramatic and some are mundane. They are all worth telling because they are ours. They could easily be yours. They are about people the same as you, no more extraordinary or mundane.

You don't have to write a book to tell your story. There are plenty of ways to tell your truth, whether you run a business or not. You don't even have to publish it if you don't want. Modern tools mean you don't have to ask permission. There are no gatekeepers left. You can still build a following by writing on your own blog, on Medium or Substack. Let YouTube, TikTok or Instagram be your playground if you'd rather do video. There are unlimited audiences and your experience and outlook to share with the world. As I write this at the end of February 2023 on the day my grandson is born, I have an idea for my next book. So you? What are you waiting for?

What's Next?

A few months and a number of delays including a banquet of COVID and a side serving of bacterial infection after I finished writing the main text of the book, I'm left with the question, what happens now? I never intended this to be a "how to", I was happy to have the stories speak for themselves. I wanted you to read about the people I featured and think, "yeah, I have something to say." But then, say what? And how?

It's not always easy to just sit down at a computer or with a pen and paper and write. Even the greatest writers produce shitty first drafts. They all stare at that blank page and think "I haven't got a clue what I'm doing." You could spend a day or two writing and think, "This is trash, I can't publish it." You could still be thinking, "surely no-one interested in what I have to say?"

Well...YOU. ARE. NOT. ALONE.

Welcome to the world of business ownership. Our dilemma is that we're constantly told to talk about ourselves in our marketing. That puts constant pressure on us to perform in a way that many of us think isn't natural and that isn't "us." But it's quite possible to tell your story in a way that is completely "you" that you can be comfortable with. You just have to work it out.

So I came up with a guide, a system to help you get things out of your head and onto paper or whatever medium you choose to get you started. The idea is that once you go through this, you'll have a bank of ideas about the stories you can tell and a plan to connect with your audience.

How to write about yourself when you have no idea where to start.

I can remember in my twenties, I desperately wanted to be a writer. I was a little confused about what I wanted to write and couldn't decide between history and short stories because a novel was too high a mountain to climb. I sat with my notebook, waiting for the perfect phrase to drop. And nothing happened, of course. My total output between the ages of 22 and 35? One short story. Slim pickings indeed. What's more, I wrote it in French because English was a bit too personal. I've lost it now, but I have notes on the other things I wrote. They were not good.

When I started translating in my late thirties, I thought I'd found a way of satisfying my writing fantasy even though I was using other people's words to do it. Yep, cheating. For years, I found talking and writing about myself an absolute nightmare. Writing about and for others was fine, but me? A hellhole of trouble.

But in the end, I worked it out. I found a system. I can't say it was always easy because some self-reflection was involved, but I came out the other end. So congratulations to you on taking the first step! Let's get into it.

You're about to discover a simple process for getting things out of your head and onto paper that will give you a different, more confident way of talking about yourself in your marketing.

Unless they are imbued with a Trump-sized ego, human beings are very good at thinking they are insignificant. We say to ourselves, "Why would anyone care about what I have to say?" We think our lives are unremarkable because we live them. The events are what we experience day-to-day. We think everyone else's lives must be more exciting.

I mentioned Neil Gaiman's anecdote about Neil Armstrong in the section about imposter syndrome. If the first man on the Moon thought he was insignificant, there's hope for us all.

So where do you start? What's the process for finally putting this stuff to bed?

You're going to need a pen and paper. They work better for this than a computer screen for this type of exercise. Research strongly suggests that we process ideas better when we use a pen and paper and my unscientific and totally anecdotal evidence corroborates that.

Step one: Clearing the head trash

This starts with one almighty caveat, I am not a mental health professional. I'm just talking about what worked for me. It may well be your experience and your background is different, so much of what I'm going to say here is general and not specific to any particular case.

Let's start with the annoying things that get in the way of us being who we want to be. They can be best described as "resistance." Steven Pressfield goes into this in great detail in books like *The War of Art*. I recommend you read that one, it's not very long, but it's very powerful.

We think we're not very good at writing, speaking or getting our point across. We think people will judge us. That's simply human nature; we grow up being judged or thinking we'll be judged. But, ironically perhaps, we think no one will read or watch if we publish. Schroedinger's judge, perhaps.

I can only repeat here the best advice I've ever been given. When you first start to write, speak into a microphone or talk to a camera, no one is looking and no one is listening to you.

And that's a good thing. That way, you can give yourself permission to write or say what the hell you like.

WRITING SOMETHING DOWN DOES NOT MEAN YOU HAVE TO PUBLISH IT. IT IS ALWAYS YOUR FIRST DRAFT

But write it down or say it, you must. You can't edit what's in your head. What you write or say at first will probably be terrible, and that's fine. When my floodgates opened, I wrote 20,000 words in three weeks. Some of it will stay on my hard drive locked up forever and some, after consideration, I don't think is so bad and it's ended up in this book.

It's never as bad as you think and no one will ever see. Just get started. If I've learned anything over the last couple of years, it's that people do care about real stories. It's the small, every day and sometimes vulnerable stories that sell.

Fundraising letters always feature case studies of things the organisation has done and not long letters of logical reasons why people would want to give money.

Washing powder ads haven't changed in my entire lifetime and they're the same everywhere in the world. Little Johnny forgot his dirty sports kit needed washing the night before a big game. Of course, the washing powder comes through and wins the day. These ads work because they encapsulate little scenes of life. Little Johnny has a terrible memory.

You can't move on the internet for storytelling podcasts, The Moth is first among them. You hear funny stories and sad ones; some mark you and some you wouldn't give more than two seconds to, but they are what make us exist as humans.

Let's be clear, there's a good deal of vulnerability involved here, so not having that pressure to publish is the greatest antidote to the fear of being found out.

And remember that you should never publish anything that you don't feel comfortable publishing anyway. No one will ever know what's on your hard disk or in your notebook. A good part of this exercise is all about making you feel better about yourself. I found writing stuff down to be cathartic. Go on, get hold of those limiting beliefs and wring their necks.

Step Two: Mapping your life out

This is the process of writing down as much as you can remember of everything that has ever happened to you. NO KIDDING. To do it properly, it'll take time. So take your weapon of choice, a spreadsheet, a Trello board or even some sheets of paper that you stick together and divide your life up into sections, old school.

This is your life, I suppose you know it quite well. You can write as little or as much as you feel comfortable with but the deeper you go, the richer the experience is likely to be.

Break it down into small manageable chunks of 3 to 7 years. If it's less, significant change becomes more difficult to detect and more, it all becomes a bit unmanageable. The number of sections will vary, of course, depending on how old you are but the principle holds for everyone. Don't try to do it all in one sitting because you'll miss a lot

The first time, you'll be able to remember the major

things you've been through like when you were born, went to school, got married and had kids (if you did), but the interesting stuff is in the later details you remember and what you felt.

Create a linear timeline as detailed as you can. At each stage, ask these questions.

What was your situation? Write down the outlines but find some anecdotes too. These will help you illustrate your stories later.

What challenges did you face, and how did you overcome them?

What was your job? When you were 15, you were a student, and that is relevant because it was the beginning of your learning.

Who were your mentors? Teachers?

What did you learn?

What skills did you acquire?

What were your personal victories and defeats? This might be difficult at first, but I've learnt as much from defeats as I have from victories.

What were you scared of?

What did you learn about yourself at the time and on reflection later with the benefit of hindsight?

There are many advantages to this that go way beyond your marketing. It will help you reconnect with yourself. That may sound a little woo, but it's not. There's solid science to prove that the more we know about ourselves, the happier we tend to be.

Beyond the timeline—a strangely validating experience in itself—it goes some way to countering any "I'm not significant" thoughts you may have. And it will give you a bank of stories you can draw on in the future.

These are what really make you unique. No one can take them away from you; they happened to you and no one else.

Step Three: Joining the dots

This is where it gets interesting

When I did this exercise, I had a breakthrough. I'm a copywriter now, but in the past, I've been a translator. I've lived half my adult life in France; I'm not just bilingual, I consider myself bicultural. That's one hell of an advantage in my line of work.

I've also been a travel agent and have a degree in History.

That means I'm an analyser, I deal in facts. I can sort the wood from the trees. Particularly doing this exercise. I interpret, translate and analyse. That's my superpower.

What about you? What patterns come from your timeline?

Ideally, find someone else to do this with. Perhaps another business owner but preferably, someone that doesn't know you too well. You could even do the exercise at the same time as them so you can analyse together. Ask these questions

- What are the common threads?
- How do you approach your life?
- Are you a rebel, or do you tend to go with the flow?
- Where are the turning points?
- What are the transformative experiences?
- How does that inform your work?
- What kind of business owner are you?
- What's your purpose?

I don't mean you supply this or that thing, but what is your higher-level value? What transformation, and how do you deliver it?

This will lead you to your philosophy. Call it your "why" if you like, but it's the reason you do what you do. It's what lights you up. Donald Miller calls this the internal problem you solve. What do you really do for your customers? It will also be what connects you with your them.

Imagine a Venn diagram where your customer and their problems are on one side, and you and your story are on the other. The area where they meet in the middle where your story and your prospect's problems come together is what you talk about.

I'll leave you with this

You are a business owner among many business owners. One of your main concerns is "how do I stand out?" and how do I get my prospects to buy from me and not Joe down the road?

All things being equal, there's nothing that separates you from Joe down the road. But all things aren't equal and there is everything that separates you from Joe.

You've just done the exercise. We are different because of our stories and we'd be crazy not to use them.

Acknowledgments

This book has been a long time in the making, and some could be forgiven for thinking it would never see the light of day. It's changed significantly over the last couple of years, and it's all the better for it.

I've already mentioned Vicky Quinn Fraser a few times. She may have been dismayed at my constructive procrastination at some points, but she always believed I'd get there in the end.

Sarah Silva also listened to my various states of mind and looked at the constantly changing Trello boards I used to organise everything.

I've known Dave Bradburn for what seems to be forever but we only ever worked on one project for a mutual friend a few years ago. He told me he'd not done many book covers but I think he's done pretty well. You can hire him at Opus Creative.

My beta readers made the book so much better—Brittany Herzog, who dived in despite not knowing me from Adam. Laura Hall, whom I met doing Seth Godin's altMBA and is currently writing and freshwater swimming herself across Scandinavia. She's been a wonderful cheerleader and confidence builder when I wasn't doing very well, Jacquie Landerman and Sue Bowness. Robin DuBroy, another altMBA alum whose constant encouragement and the long conversations we still have while six thousand miles apart fill me with a sense of connection. That's all I'm looking for. And finally, again, Sarah Silva, for how she's stuck with me over the years.

I interviewed many people but didn't include everyone in the book - it would have been at least twice as long had I done so. Thank you to Margo Aaron, Marcia Adair, Ash Ambirge, Ronni Bast, Caroline Betz, Louise Blackburn, Chris Brogan, Debb Cobb, Michelle Dalley, Amanda-Kay Dozanti, and Shaine Germano. Laura Hall, Amy Harrison, John Holcroft, Gillian Horan, Jo Howarth, Kira Hug, James Hutchison. Neely Khan, Kenda MacDonald, Cara Mackay, Maddy Mazzola, Fabi Paolini, Vicky Quinn Fraser, Harriet Randall, Adam Reifsteck, Marilu Revelli, Emma Roache, Gemma Roe, Claire Russell, Misty Santos, Rebecca Seal, Sarah Silva, Shay Sun, Stef Thomas, Britta Vercoutter and Sheena Whyatt. I enjoyed every one of our conversations immensely.

Many people made me a better writer, even though they may not necessarily know. Ash Ambirge (again), Margo Aaron, Laura Belgray (for her emails and a brief exchange about real Batman, Adam West), Kira Hug, Brian Clark, Sonia Simone, and so many others.

A few people helped with my sanity over the years. Not just when writing the book. Jo Howarth, Emma Roache, Claire Russell, AK Dozanti and Basil Meinie. The Copywriter Think Tank crew has been a constant source of inspiration and support.

I should mention Seth Godin, too, the altMBA and the Creatives' Workshop gave me the belief and structure to make this book what it is.

Bernadette Jiwa's books on business storytelling that got me started with this malarky in the first place, her Story Skills workshops and our conversations have been an inspiration.

Finally, I'm grateful for all the people I've spoken to worldwide in the last couple of years who've encouraged me, believed in me and made me say to myself, "yeah, I have something to say."

About the Author

This is my first book and it's been a journey. It's the fruit of experience gained over a lifetime of moving between two languages and cultures that has led me to where I am today. I have big ambitions for the future.

I wasn't always a writer, my role was to read the books writers wrote. I tried so hard to be one for years and years, but I couldn't make it happen.

Then a couple of years ago, I had a profound shift and it suddenly started working. I realised that I had something to say and my forty years as an adult had turned up some corking stories that would interest people.

I went to France straight out of University and gained a second language and a second culture. In reverse order, I've been a copywriter and translator for the last 25 years. I trained to be a teacher in a competitive exam in France. I failed by a hair's breadth, but I successfully wrote about Shakespeare in French. That's a win for me. I've been an EFL teacher and a business travel agent and got to go the Berlin six months after the wall came down in 1990. I worked in British Rail's European Passenger Travel Office in London in the days before the Channel Tunnel when we sent trains to the boats in Dover and Folkestone and I was the Information Officer at the Franco-British Chamber of Commerce in Paris.

Oh, and I worked in a paint and decorating shop in my

London suburb, I had a paper round when I was at school and I did a milk round when I was 13. That was probably illegal even in 1971.

So here we are, a *bona fide* writer with a book under his arm. And I'm going to write more. I'm just getting started.

13 things about me.

- I pass for French in France. I'm learning Spanish and have an 1800-day streak and counting on Duolingo. But the best way to learn is with a teacher. I'm proud of my French accent in Spanish.
- I gained a love for French cinema, steak tartare and the Breton coastline from my 20 years as an ex-pat.
- I'm originally a London boy, but through a long and romantic sequence of events, I came to rest in Somerset.
- I didn't pass my driving test until I was 37 and learned in a left-hand drive car.
- I have an unhealthy interest in seventeenth-century millenarians and experimental and leftfield music.
- I'm a fiendish devil's advocate who will see opportunities in your business that you won't necessarily see because you're too close to it.
- A friend who shall remain nameless sent me down a home reno show rabbit hole from whence I have yet to emerge.
- It's probably an unhealthy obsession, but I plan to learn some woodworking skills so I can handle a table saw just like the people in those shows.

- I make a mean onion tart (that used to surprise the French!)
- I've also got a degree in History and French.
- I used to be a wholesale birdseed trader.
- I may look older, but my mind hasn't made 40 yet.
- I have no intention of retiring. I have too many things to say to the world. What's good enough for Mel Brooks is good enough for me.

How To Get In Touch

I can remember a time when if you had a record played on the radio, your entire address was read out for the nation to hear. I had one played for my brother once and we got a letter from someone offering us a recording of it. Who new a compact cassette and a recorder with a microphone taped to the radio could give you a business in 1972? (Kids? Ask your parents).

There many was of contacting people today, but giving out an address on national radio isn't one of them.

Addresses on the internet are so transient so there is no guarantee that if I give you a website today it will still be there by the time you get to it.

I have no agent (yet) so I'm going out on a limb saying that LinkedIn will be around for a while. You can find me @mikegarnercopywriter on there. All other media sees me as @mikegarner.

Although you can email me at mike@storiesthatmatter.co and tell me how you might start telling your story. A few sentences or a bunch of paragraphs, I'd love to hear what you do with this stuff. Just between you and me.

www.ingramcontent.com/pod-product-compliance
Lightning Source LLC
Chambersburg PA
CBHW030509210326
41597CB00013B/843